JULES OLITSKI

KENWORTH MOFFETT JULES

OLITSKI

HARRY N. ABRAMS, INC., PUBLISHERS, NEW YORK

Editor: Donald Goddard
Designer: Bob McKee
Picture Research: Christopher de B. Sweet

Library of Congress Cataloging in Publication Data

Moffett, Kenworth.
    Jules Olitski.

    Bibliography: p. 234
    Includes index.
    1.   Olitski, Jules, 1922-   2.   Artists—United
States—Biography.   I.   Olitski, Jules, 1922-
N6537.038M63   709'.2'4   80-21143
ISBN 0-8109-1403-4

Illustrations © 1981 Harry N. Abrams, Inc.

Printed and bound in Japan

Title page: 1. *Pink Alert*. 1966.
Water-miscible acrylic on canvas, 113 × 80".
The Corcoran Gallery of Art, Washington, D. C.
Gift of the Friends of The Corcoran Gallery of Art

Acknowledgments

Lois and George de Menil made this book possible.
I am indebted to the following people who gave
generously of their time to help me prepare it: Jules
Olitski, Kristina Olitski, Richard Ziello, David Mirvish,
Clement Greenberg, and Deborah Emerson. The
André Emmerich Gallery and M. Knoedler & Co. in
New York as well as the Kasmin Gallery in London
gave me indispensable help too. I especially want
to mention Anne Freedman and Marion Moffett of
Knoedler's and Dorsey Waxter of the Emmerich
Gallery. I also want to thank my editor,
Donald Goddard.

For Kay

CONTENTS

Errata

Please note that the works illustrated in plates 4, 6, 7, 13, 14, 15, and 16 are in the artist's collection, and the one in plate 5 is in the Uffizi, Florence, Italy. The painting in plate 134 is in the collection of Janice and Clement Greenberg. Plate 212 shows Olitski and his mother, Anna; plate 216 shows Olitski at 21; and plate 217 shows Chaim Gross's class at the Educational Alliance, New York.

ONE THE DEVELOPMENT OF OLITSKI'S PAINTING

Jules Olitski studied art at the National Academy of Design in New York in the early 1940s. While the portraits he did then show a certain expressionist emphasis, they are rooted in the Baroque tradition of rich paint handling and chiaroscuro (pls. 4–7). It was at the National Academy, and even more in museums, that he learned the full range of the old master devices—scumbling, glazes, impasto—which he continues to use today. By 1950, though, Olitski came to feel that he had to unlearn this elaborate painting culture—unlearn it in order to discover its relevance for modern art. He was ambitious. He wanted to make something new, personal. Living in Paris and feeling oppressed by what seemed to him a too fully assimilated training, Olitski began to ask what all that he had learned had to do with him, with his own feelings. He abandoned the French modernist tradition in which he was working at that point—Bonnard, Braque, Matisse. He also gave up the romantic, Rembrandtesque portraiture he had been doing on the side. For a time he stopped visiting museums. He began to paint blindfolded. The Surrealists had already tried similar unorthodox procedures in the effort to escape their own expectations and assumptions: the habits of hand and eye learned in the schools and museums. Relying on impulses and motor rhythms—and not at all on the contours of nature—Surrealists such as Masson and Miró achieved a new, freer kind of drawing. Sometimes they would find or confirm "unconscious" images in these scribbles and meanderings so as to draw into the picture something of the rich shape vocabulary and suggestiveness of nature. But as this open drawing developed it called for some greater resistance, some stronger challenge to the rhythmic movement of the hand. If this resistance could no longer come from the visible world then it had to come from matter itself, matter as paint on the picture's

2. Joan Miró. *Painting*. 1930.
Oil on canvas, 59 × 88 5/8".
Private collection

3. Paul Klee. *Fearsome Animals (Grausame Tiere)*. 1926.
Watercolor on paper, 18 1/4 × 12 1/4". Private collection

surface. So, such artists as Klee (pl. 3) and Miró moved toward a rough painterly linearism in the late 1930s, a mode that became important both in the United States and in Europe in the 1940s and '50s. This is the context of Olitski's blindfold paintings (pls. 13–17). Though his results were not especially interesting or distinguished, this way of working must have had a liberating effect on him, personally and artistically. And the Surrealist attitude of free playfulness would work for him later on.

When he returned from Europe in 1951, Olitski tried another novel approach to picture making, which, looking back, now seems prophetic. The blindfold pictures had at first been abstract, but became more figurative, if in a schematic way (the results were not unlike those of the European CoBrA painters—such as Karel Appel and Asger Jorn). The new "drawing-board" pictures were completely abstract, and Olitski now began not with a procedure but with a layout or configuration (pls.18–20, 24):

. . . one day in an art classroom, I was struck by the *look* of a certain drawing board. There were any number of drawing boards on tables and leaning against the walls. Now, I had seen drawing boards for a good part of my life without giving them any special notice. Why I noticed one that day and one in particular is beyond me. And why I thought it looked like a painting or had in it the makings of a painting is also beyond me. You know, of course, what a used drawing board comes to look like with its lines and blots and drips. I began to look at all the drawing boards in the classroom and some struck me as *pictorially* better than others and those I chose to use as "models" for painting. I took three or four to my studio. That was how the drawing board pictures began.[1]

Seen as a painting, a used drawing board makes the center, the traditional locus of meaning and importance, blank, dead-pan; while lines and markings, the result of strokes running off the paper placed in the middle of the board, appear only

5. *Self-portrait*. Early 1940s.
Oil on canvas, 30 × 40''.
Collection of the artist

4. *Self-portrait*. Early 1940s.
Oil on canvas, dimensions
and whereabouts unknown

6. *Portrait of Sidney Dickinson, N.A.* 1941.
Oil on canvas, dimensions
and whereabouts unknown

7. *Portrait of Robert White*. Early
1940s. Oil on canvas, dimensions
and whereabouts unknown

8. *Girl with Fan*. 1946.
Oil on canvas, 23 1/4 × 19 3/4".
Collection of the artist

12. *Portrait of a Girl*. 1947.
Oil on canvas, dimensions and
whereabouts unknown

9. *Woman with Roses and a Dog*.
c. 1946. Oil on canvas, 39 × 29".
Collection of the artist

10. *Still Life*. 1946.
Oil on canvas, 29 3/4 × 23 3/8".
Collection of the artist

11. *Black Stockings*. 1946.
Oil on canvas, 20 × 24".
Collection of the artist

15. *Untitled.* 1949–51.
Oil on paper, now destroyed

16. *Untitled.* 1949–51.
Oil on paper, now destroyed

13. *Untitled.* 1949–51.
Oil on paper, now destroyed

14. *Untitled.* 1949–51.
Oil on paper, now destroyed

17. *Untitled.* 1949–51.
Oil on paper, now destroyed

18. *Drawing Board*. 1951.
Oil on canvas, dimensions and
whereabouts unknown

20. *Drawing Board #4*. 1953.
Oil on board, 36 × 29 1/2".
Collection of the artist

19. *Drawing Board (White)*. c. 1952–53.
Oil on canvas, 37 × 37". Collection of the artist

at the edges, creating a kind of internal frame. If they are not impressive in themselves, the drawing-board pictures are certainly remarkable given Olitski's later development, and they also show how up-to-date—if in European terms—he was at this point.

The Surrealists had introduced a freer kind of drawing, but to accomplish this they had to think first in terms of a flat foreground and a flat background. This way of thinking goes back to collage, but the Surrealists were more explicit; they made the foreground line and the background "field." When in the 1940s painting became painterly, denser, and therefore flatter, or flat in a tactile way, the Surrealist dichotomy between figure and ground increasingly came to be resolved in favor of one or the other. So in the late 1940s and '50s in both Europe and America there were two main tendencies— painterly linearism, as in Jackson Pollock's paintings (pl. 23) or in Olitski's blindfold pictures, and "field" painting, which stresses the ground of the abstract Surrealist picture. The latter was the approach of Clyfford Still, Barnett Newman (pl. 21), and Mark Rothko, who grasped new possibilities here for scale and color. In Europe this tendency emphasized matter and texture; the leading figure was Jean Dubuffet (pl. 22). Both European and American field painting were oriented to a serial image, which in America was usually abstract, but in Europe it was often a flat, tactile equivalent of the visible world that had ironic or symbolic connotations (a wall, a door, a tabletop, a landscape seen from above, a child's drawing).[2]

While in Europe Olitski sought out the work of Jean Dubuffet because of an article he had read by the critic Clement Greenberg. Dubuffet was the best painter in Europe at that point, and Olitski speaks of his influence as "liberating." Recently Olitski said that the nature of this influence lay "in the ways

21. Barnett Newman. *Onement No. 6.* 1953.
Oil on canvas, 102 × 120".
Frederick Weisman Family Collection, Beverly Hills, Calif.

22. Jean Dubuffet. *High Heels.* 1946.
Oil on canvas, 21 5/8 × 21 1/2".
Collection Sidney and Harriet Janis.
Gift to The Museum of Modern Art, New York

23. Jackson Pollock. *Number 1, 1948*. 1948.
Oil on canvas, 68 × 104"
The Museum of Modern Art, New York

24. *Untitled*. 1952. Spackle, acrylic resin, and dry pigments on canvas, dimensions and whereabouts unknown

25. *Untitled.* c. 1953–55.
Spackle, acrylic resin, and dry pigments on
canvas, dimensions and whereabouts unknown

26. *Untitled.* 1954.
Oil on canvas, dimensions and whereabouts unknown

he made the surface *count.*"³ Seeing the quality of Dubuffet's pictures meant seeing how an emphasis on the material
unity of the whole flat surface offered a new pictorial feeling.
The drawing-board pictures reflect this perception in Olitski's
work for the first time, but in a way that is very much his own.

The use of a model that coincides exactly with the rectangle
of the canvas, the small scale, the thick paint, and the tendency
toward neutrals or monochrome are all features that Olitski's
drawing-board pictures share with European field abstraction or "matter painting." On the other hand, Olitski's paintings
are not images and are completely abstract in intent; knowing
that they have been done from drawing boards adds nothing
to the experiencing of these pictures. The best of them are good,
even original, but without being very bold or large in feeling.

Between 1954 and 1957, Olitski painted a series of small
black and white pictures which seem like semi-abstract landscapes (pl. 27). He then began a series of paintings in 1957
that were the reverse of the drawing-board "portraits," but no
less prophetic, still eschewing spectrum colors, perhaps in
reaction to the bright Fauve-like hues he had employed in his
Paris years. Olitski caused thick, plastered areas of white
impasto to swell up out of the centers of grayed and generally
heavily painted surfaces (pls. 29–42). The pictures were made
of spackle, paint, colored pigments, and acrylic resins, which
create a viscous density far exceeding the normal facture of
oil painting. Colors are earth tones or cool charcoal grays.
Often faintly figurative, at least two of these paintings show a
standing nude seen from behind (pls. 30, 31). Sometimes the
colors suggest flesh tones and a few of the pictures are distinctly landscape- or portrait-like in feeling. These features have
reminded some writers of postwar European paintings, those
of Fautrier (pl. 32) and De Staël.⁴ The impasto pictures do
seem somehow French, and out of the mainstream of American

28. *Demikov*. 1957.
Oil on board, 24 × 18 1/2''.
Collection of the artist

27. *Black and White Composition*. 1955.
Spackle, acrylic resin, and dry pigments on canvas, 23 1/2 × 35 1/2''.
Collection of the artist

29. *Untitled*. 1956–58.
Spackle, acrylic resin, and
dry pigments on canvas, dimensions
and whereabouts unknown

30. *Untitled (Nude)*. c. 1957–58.
Spackle, acrylic resin, and dry pigments on canvas,
29 1/2 × 12''.
Collection of the artist

31. *Brown Figure*. 1957.
Spackle, acrylic resin, and dry pigments on canvas,
21 5/8 × 18''.
Collection of the artist

abstraction as it was developing in those years. But perhaps they are best seen in the light of Olitski's own ambitions. In a recent letter he wrote:

If you want to know the true inspiration and influence (apart from the example of Dubuffet) upon my matter paintings—it comes essentially out of Rembrandt and to some extent Goya as well as Hals, Titian, Veronese. I was trying to extend Rembrandt's use of flowing paint, his chiaroscuro, and just as much, his impasto into modern painting; for the most part abstract. (Perhaps a vain ambition, but there it was and to some extent, still is.) In fact, while I was a doctoral candidate at N.Y.U. around the year 1955 or 1956 the creative thesis I proposed (it was to involve a dozen or so paintings) was exactly that, the "Rembrandt notion." I remember this very well because my professor jeered at what he took to be my arrogance in daring to couple my name with the great master. That incident, fortunately for me, made me decide to quit the doctoral program.[5]

Several of the impasto pictures are indeed like Rembrandt portraits in that the thickest impasto coincides both with the approximate center, or more usually slightly above the center, of the picture and the area of greatest highlight. More generally, they show a subtlety of chiaroscuro and a sensuality and complexity of paint handling reminiscent of the old masters admired by Olitski, but done with the continuous material unity of the flat rectangular surface very much in mind. It is characteristic that once he had gained a grip on modern painting, Olitski turned immediately back to the old masters he loved. The results were mature, realized pictures, some of them as good as or even better than most European abstraction done during those years, the context in which they should be seen. They don't compare in quality with the best American work of the period, but in the next few years Olitski would add to his repertoire color and large scale, features that were particularly important in American abstraction. Once he had

32. Jean Fautrier. *La Boite Vide.*
Oil on canvas, 10 5/8 × 13 3/4".
Private collection, Paris

33. *Untitled*. c. 1958.
Spackle, acrylic resin, and dry
pigments on canvas, 36 × 23 1/2''.
Collection of the artist

34. *Untitled*. 1958.
Spackle, acrylic resin, and dry
pigments on canvas, 30 × 20''.
Collection of the artist

35. *Untitled*. c. 1958.
Spackle, acrylic resin, and dry
pigments on canvas, 10 × 14''.
Collection of the artist

36. *Model of the Photo Annual*. 1958.
Spackle, acrylic resin, and dry
pigments on canvas, 60 × 73 1/2''.
Collection of the artist

37. *Ballet Dancer Waiting*. 1959.
·Spackle, acrylic resin, and dry pigments on canvas, 50 × 41″. Collection of the artist

38. *Lucy Lubric*. 1959.
Spackle, acrylic resin, and dry pigments on canvas, 72 × 84″. Collection of the artist

developed these features in his own way, he would again turn back to the old masters. By that time, however, he would be one of America's leading painters.

An interesting feature of the impasto paintings is the way Olitski has used charcoal or touches of dark paint to reinforce and "pictorialize" the actual shadows created by the high areas of impasto. Also, two of the most remarkable of these pictures relate to Olitski's later work: *Ten O'Clock*, 1959 (pl. 39), with its lighter key, brighter color, and blob-shaped ellipses, points to his stain paintings of the next few years; and *Demikov One,* 1957 (pl. 40), like the earlier drawing-board paintings and much of his later work, empties the center of incident. It is important to note that both of these pictures are based on contingencies suggested by paint itself and the rectangle and not by any initial or discovered image.

At the end of 1959, Olitski made an abrupt shift in style that suddenly aligned his art with what was then the most advanced American painting. His canvases became larger, their surfaces stripped bare of impasto or paint texture of any kind (pls. 43–50). Prismatic colors soaked into the canvas appeared as bright biomorphic-looking shapes with sharp undulating contours usually placed off-center on a black ground (*Mushroom Joy*, 1959; *Potsy*, 1960, pl. 50). This was a very different kind of painting for Olitski. It had little to do with subtleties of tone or variations of value, let alone relief-like effects, but a great deal to do with vivid contour, placement, and color as hue. Above all it was now scale and color, two features neglected by, or, more properly, unavailable to early twentieth-century abstractionists, that assumed the main expressive emphasis.

A few years earlier, Helen Frankenthaler, then Morris Louis (pl. 58), then Kenneth Noland (pl. 57), then Friedel Dzubas (pl. 51), and then the Canadian painter Jack Bush had com-

39. *Ten O'Clock.* 1959.
Spackle, acrylic resin, and dry pigments on canvas, 36 3/4 × 35 1/4".
Collection of the artist

40. *Demikov One*. 1957.
Spackle, acrylic resin, and dry pigments on
canvas, 37 × 37".
Collection of the artist

41. *Triumph of Wentworth*. 1958.
Spackle, acrylic resin, and dry pigments on
canvas, 36 1/4 × 28 7/8".
Collection of the artist

42. *Late Madness of Wentworth*. 1958.
Spackle, acrylic resin, and dry pigments
on canvas, 60 × 48".
Collection of the artist

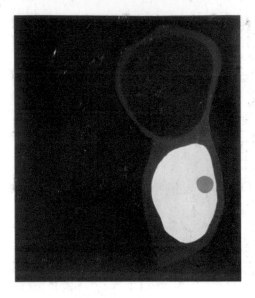

43. *Necessary Light*. 1959.
Oil-miscible acrylic on canvas,
80 1/2 × 68 1/2".
Collection of the artist

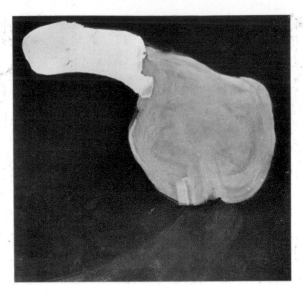

44. *Fanny C*. 1960.
Dye on canvas, 80 × 84 1/2".
Collection of the artist

45. *Suavium*. 1960.
Dye on canvas, 80 × 108".
Collection of the artist

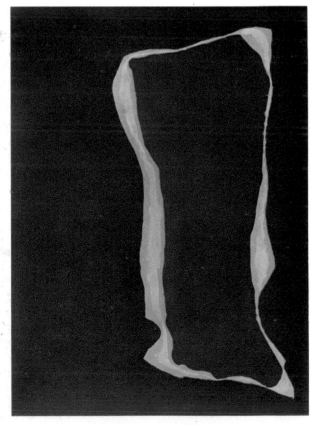

46. *The Blush*. 1960.
Oil-miscible acrylic on canvas, 108 × 80".
Collection of the artist

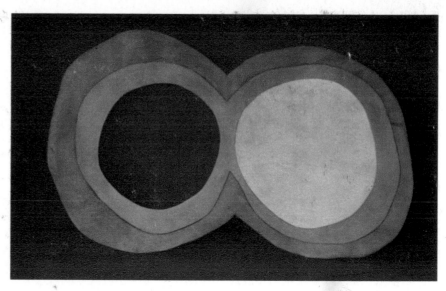

47. *Osculum Silence*. 1960.
Dye on canvas, 80 × 108''.
(destroyed)

48. *Lucy's Fantasy*. 1960.
Oil-miscible acrylic on canvas, 79 × 125''.
Collection of the artist

49. *Untitled*. 1960.
Oil-miscible acrylic on canvas, 80 7/8 × 135''.
Collection of the artist

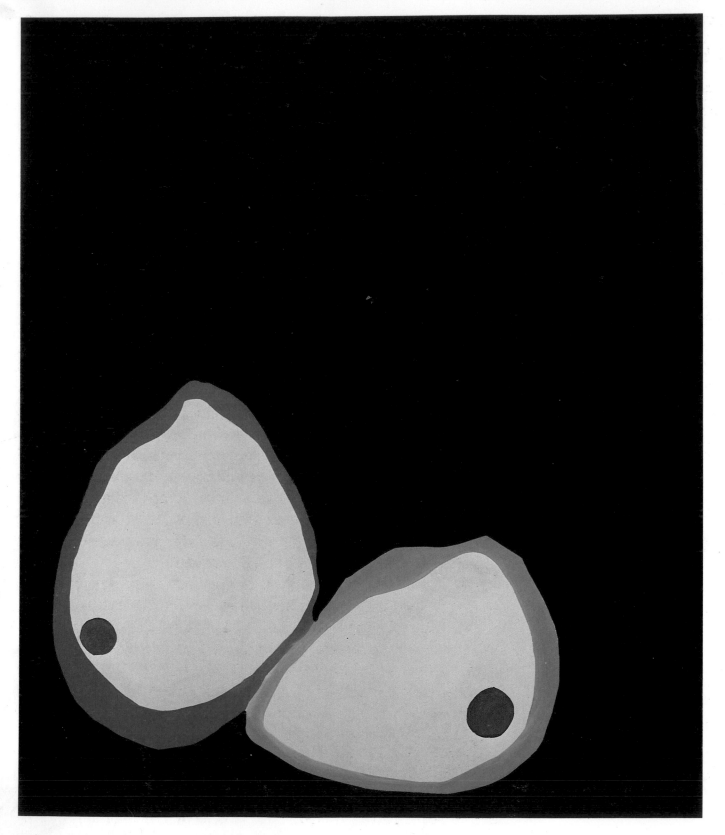

50. *Potsy*. 1960. Oil-miscible acrylic on canvas, 80 × 68 1/4″. Collection of the artist

51. Friedel Dzubas. *Dawn*. 1960.
Oil on canvas, 94 1/2 × 72".
Museum of Fine Arts, Boston, Mass.
Edwin E. Jack Fund

52. Morris Louis. *Beth Ayin*. 1958.
Acrylic on canvas, 91 × 129".
Collection Mr. and Mrs. S. I. Newhouse, Jr., New York

bined Jackson Pollock's staining and its literal immediacy of surface with the simplified layout first developed in the work of Rothko, Newman, and Still. Olitski's shift to this kind of thinned down, large-scale, and boldly designed color picture seems to have been the result of his experience of New York painting. But his development at this time, although accelerated, remained continuous. He used bright, prismatic colors in his last impasto paintings,[6] and the new pictures, like the immediately preceding ones, showed areas of light emerging from a dark ground. The earliest of the new pictures look like abstractions of the last impasto pictures. Also, unlike Louis and Noland, who thinned their paint down to achieve a watercolor-like airiness, Olitski seemed to be searching for another kind of thin paint application which, without impasto, would continue to evoke density and fullness. It was this intention, I think, that lay behind his experimentation at this time with different paint mediums (dyes and enamel paint over dyes; pls. 44, 45, 47), many of which either turned out to be impermanent or produced flat, poster-like surfaces with an opaquely brittle look. (Many of these have been destroyed.)

These technical difficulties probably led Olitski, late in 1961, to adopt the staining already used by Frankenthaler, Louis, Noland, and Dzubas: thin water-based acrylic pigment which would soak through the unprimed canvas fabric. Like them he also used areas of bare canvas to point up the identification of color and support by stressing the lack of textural change between painted and unpainted areas. The pictures were immediately in a very different, much higher key; color was bright and assertive. These so-called "core" pictures (pls. 53–56, 59–61), done between 1962 and 1963, are Olitski's first great works. A painting such as *Born in Snovsk* (pl. 61), at the Art Institute of Chicago, is one of the masterworks of stain painting.

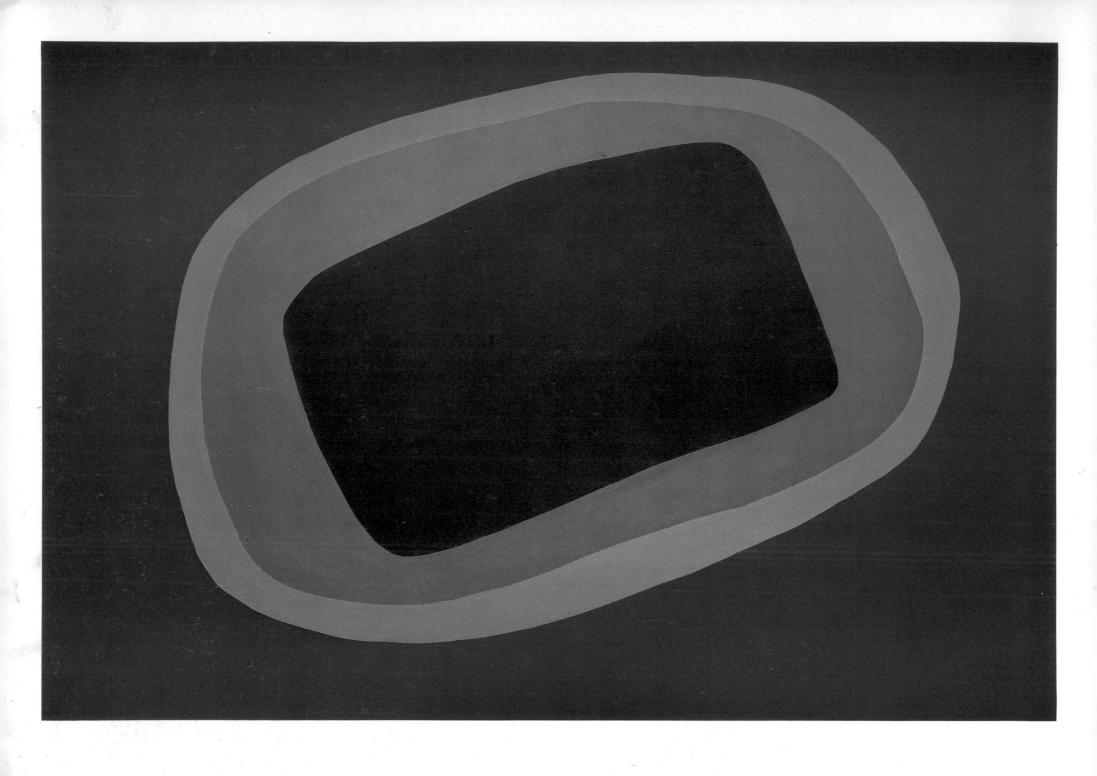

53. *Ishtar Bra*. 1961. Water-miscible acrylic on canvas, 80 × 120''. Collection of the artist

54. *House of Orange*. 1961–62. Water-miscible acrylic on canvas, 80 × 91 7/8". Collection of the artist

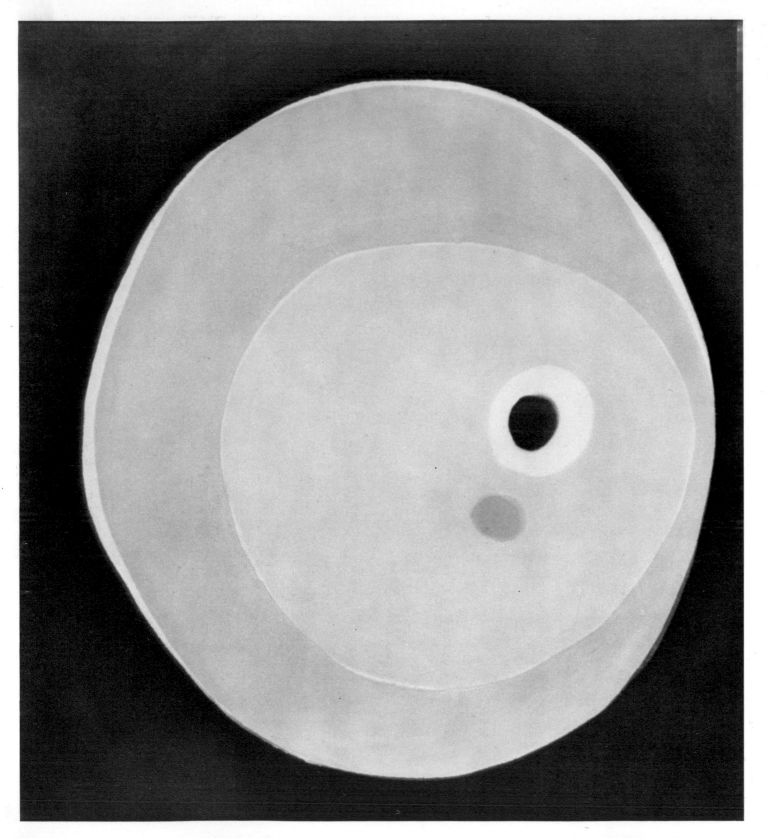

55. *Pink Love—Homage to Ken Noland*. 1962. Oil-miscible acrylic on canvas, 44 × 40″. Collection of the artist

56. *After Five*. 1961. Acrylic resin on canvas, 92 1/2 × 93 1/2''. Collection Mr. and Mrs. David Mirvish, Toronto, Ont.

Staining automatically gives a continuous material flatness, but unlike dripping or pouring, it does not dictate any specific kind of figuration. The illusion appears disembodied and can even seem to be slightly behind the physical nap and weave of the canvas, especially if the color is pale and washy. The tendency of the stain painters, then, has been to find a design or layout that presses the illusion still closer to the surface. Noland did this with geometric design, thereby identifying areas of color as closely as possible with the support—which itself is geometric—and reinforcing the effect of staining. This makes the painting pure, sheer surface, and gives the whole a weightless feeling. Conversely, in his Unfurleds (pl. 58), Louis used emphatic, cutting edges and prismatic contrasts (e.g., blue against yellow) to give a sense of plastic weight and force to the whole. Olitski too wanted this weight, and the cutting, visually crackling edges that one finds in Olitski's early stain pictures appear already in his work in 1959.[7] The core pictures also share with Louis's Unfurleds an openness of composition; the inside implies expansion beyond the frame or, alternately, the whole picture seems like a framing of a larger whole. But with the Unfurleds, the enframement "holds" the interior tautly, even while it allows it to expand generously, while in Olitski's pictures there is a tendency for the inside to seem squeezed by the (often vertical) rectangle, which gives a feeling of jamming and density under pressure.

Like Noland, Olitski favored concentric configurations that nowhere echoed the rectangle's edges; but while Noland stuck to centered circles, Olitski used concentricity as a way to anchor the whole surface or field—to give a sense of interior— *without* succumbing to the formality of geometry or symmetry. This "pinning" allows the edges of an open, expanding field to flap free, as it were, while retaining a sense of completeness or focus. This in turn allowed Olitski to establish the

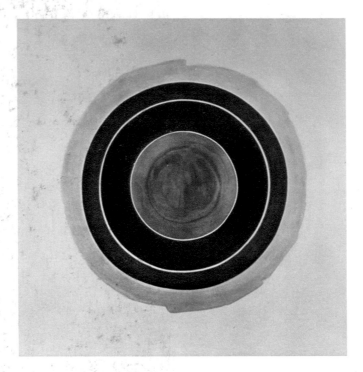

57. Kenneth Noland. *Ember*. 1960. Oil on canvas, 70 1/2 × 70". Collection Dr. and Mrs. M. Wallace Friedman, San Francisco, Calif.

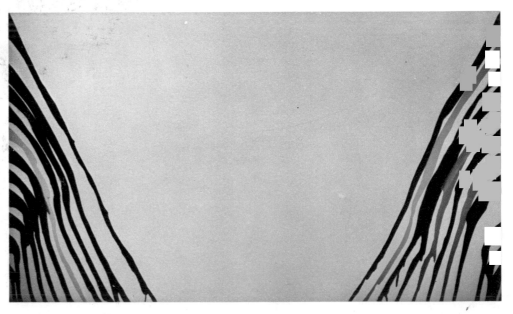

58. Morris Louis. *Ksi*. 1960. Acrylic on canvas, 104 × 172". Folkwang Museum, Essen, West Germany

59. *Cleopatra Flesh*. 1962.
Oil-miscible acrylic on canvas, 104 × 90".
The Museum of Modern Art, New York. Gift of G. David Thompson (by exchange)

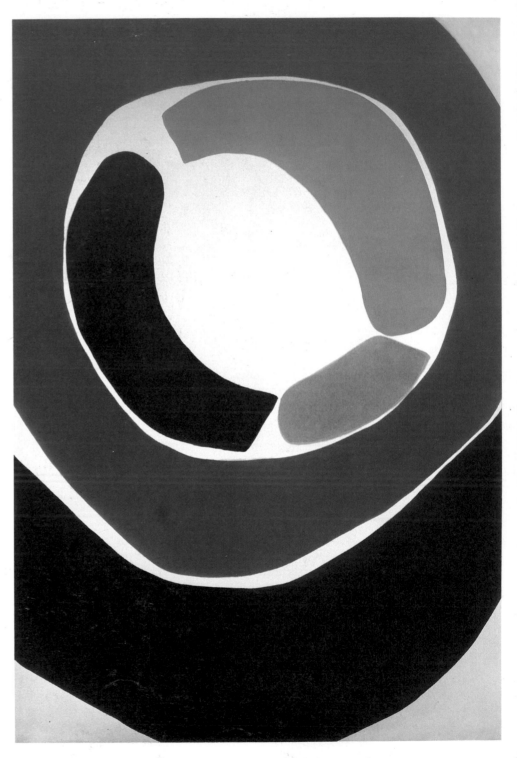

60. *Ino Delight*. 1962.
Water-miscible acrylic on canvas, 92 × 55 7/8''.
The Norman Mackenzie Art Gallery, University of Regina, Regina, Sask.

61. *Born in Snovsk*. 1963.
Water-miscible acrylic on canvas, 132 × 90''.
The Art Institute of Chicago, Chicago, Ill. Gift of the Ford Foundation

62. *Yaksi Juice*. 1963. Oil-miscible acrylic and varnish on canvas, 66 × 80''. Collection of the artist

proportions without confining the inside and strictly on the basis of the inside. So, for example, Olitski, unlike Noland, was not limited to the square. The organization of his pictures was looser and more flexible, which opened possibilities for "cropping," that is, for determining the size and shape of the picture after it was painted.

The family of shapes in these pictures—funky ovoids, whimsical ellipses, small dots, and lopsided doughnut forms—are reminiscent of Miró and Gottlieb, but they are very much Olitski's own and, indeed, had already appeared in some of the impasto pictures (and would appear later in his sculpture). In fact, they are based on photographs of female nudes and breasts that Olitski had used as "models" as early as the impasto pictures.

There is a sense in which the core pictures succeed *despite* the natural properties of stain.[8] Their graphic vividness can seem to put color in second place [9] or to limit it too much to contrasts. The "falling curtain" pictures, which start in 1963, may be a response to this perception. In *Fatal Plunge Lady* (pl. 68), a flood of color rolls downward toward the bottom edge but does not quite attain it. In most of these paintings the flow is from the upper left to the lower right corner. Again the composition is neither symmetrical nor balanced out in a traditional way. The concept here certainly was evolved to get more color *as color* into the picture, and it was almost surely suggested by unusual off-center croppings of the later core pictures.

The falling curtain pictures are not broadly "anchored" like the core pictures but delicately "pinned" with small complete elements, often only a dot in the lower corner. This "balances" the big field, which by implication is much larger than the actual surface. It breaks in, across, and down a vertical surface, pushing toward completeness which is "symbolized," ex-

63. *Wet Heat Co.* 1963.
Oil-miscible acrylic on canvas, 80 1/8 × 92".
Collection of the artist

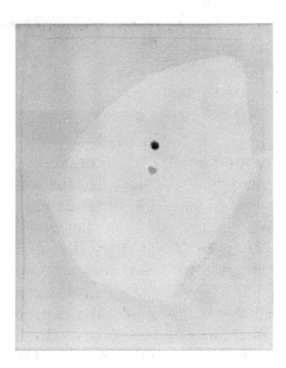

64. *Fatal Plunge*. 1963.
Oil-miscible acrylic on canvas, 97 × 68''.
Collection of the artist

65. *Beautiful Bald Woman*. 1963.
Whereabouts unknown

66. *Stamp Act*. 1963.
Oil-miscible acrylic on canvas, 28 × 22''.
Collection of the artist

67. *V*. 1963.
Oil-miscible acrylic on canvas, 64 × 64''.
Collection of the artist

68. *Fatal Plunge Lady*. 1963.
Oil-miscible acrylic on canvas, 100 × 72''. Kasmin, Ltd., London, England

69. *Pizzazz*. 1963.
Oil-miscible acrylic on canvas,
26 1/8 × 19 7/8".
Collection of the artist

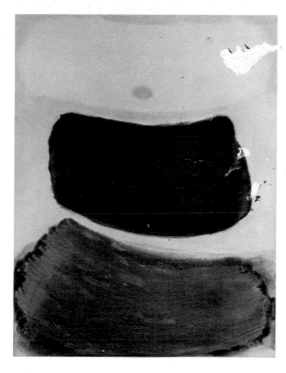

70. *Sugar Daddy*. 1963.
Oil-miscible acrylic on canvas,
36 1/4 × 27 7/8".
Collection of the artist

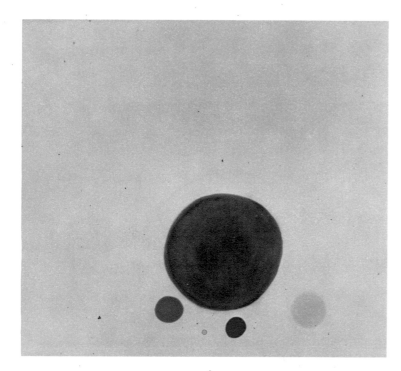

71. *Monkey Woman*. 1964.
Water-miscible acrylic on canvas, 66 × 72".
Collection Mr. and Mrs. David Mirvish, Toronto, Ont.

pressed by the tiny shapes at the lower corner. It is as if Olitski wants to eliminate predetermined ordering as much as possible, as if he were rebelling against the clear edges and symmetrical design that he found in Noland and Louis. As with his impasto pictures and later work, the nature of the material, in this case the liquid properties of paint, becomes the main determinant of a picture's composition, just as color now becomes the main expressive agent. Yet the still depicted, even figurative, feeling of these pictures moved Olitski to something else in the following year. The flow detaches itself from the edge and comes to dominate the entire center of the picture, crowding up against margins of raw canvas or swatches and spottings of color at the very edges, as in *Flaubert Red* (pl. 73), *Tin Lizzy Green* (pl. 72), *Deep Drag*, and others—masterpieces were frequent in 1964.

Due to the paint application—with sponges, and more often rollers that create wedge-shaped edges—pictures such as *Flaubert Red* and *Deep Drag* are full and dense, packed with color. Others relinquish density and seem like colored carpets suspended in the rectangles. The picture no longer develops outward from an anchoring shape or downward as a falling curtain, but from the inside out, with the edges of the field pushing outward in all directions. Or the field hovers free of the rectangle, sometimes bumping into it, but basically as a second, created surface with its own unity and authority, focus and completeness declared by the singleness of monochrome. This conception of a second, autonomous, roughly rectangular field, which has no final expressive shape but is so coherent and homogeneous in itself that it dominates and neutralizes the actual rectangle, has been the basis of all Olitski's subsequent work.[10]

Louis's Veils were something of a precedent. They too had a singleness of effect resulting from a broad flood of paint and

72. *Tin Lizzy Green*. 1964.
Water-miscible acrylic on canvas, 130 × 82″. Museum of Fine Arts, Boston, Mass.
Purchased with the aid of funds from the National Endowment for the Arts

73. *Flaubert Red*. 1964. Oil-miscible acrylic on canvas, 82 × 106 3/4''. First City National Bank, Houston, Tex.

74. *Hot Ticket*. 1964.
Water-miscible acrylic on canvas, 139 × 81″. Kasmin, Ltd.. London, England

75. *Polly Le Touche*. 1964. Water-miscible acrylic on canvas,
113 1/2 × 81″. Collection Mr. and Mrs. David Mirvish, Toronto, Ont.

monochrome. But Olitski used only one staining and chromatic colors.[11] (Layering would have produced brown or bronze, much like Louis's Veils.) Also he didn't anchor the field with gravity, as Louis did, and he avoided symmetry. In a picture like *Tin Lizzy Green*, a thin washy field seems both to hover and to push the playful figuration to the margins.

Olitski was not concerned to exhaust all the possibilities inherent in his 1964 "field" pictures, but instead he moved quickly in the following year to something quite different. As can be seen in some of the 1964 pictures, such as *Hot Ticket* (pl. 74) and *Tin Lizzy Green*, he wished to introduce sharp changes of hue, especially complementary changes from, say, green to red, within the field, something that is difficult to achieve by staining without creating grayed or browned transitional areas that can look muddy. (As we have noted, this is true of all layering with stain.) So he had to stick pretty much to a monochrome field created by a single application. That is, he was limited in terms of both color variation and density. These were probably the considerations that led Olitski to the spray technique. Spraying allowed him to vary the thickness of the paint even while it meant broken color in the form of tiny drops that fused in the eye or on the surface. Modulation of color into color became smoother and less disruptive.

In an abstract painting in which the materials themselves used in their literal immediacy more and more come to count as the sole expressive agents, the discovery of a new technique, a new manner of application, can mean a new style and content. This was true, for example, of Jackson Pollock's drip technique, Morris Louis's stainings, and, more recently, of Larry Poons' pourings. Olitski's spraying created a new kind of color painting, one that was closer to Louis's Veils than to Olitski's own previous stain pictures or those of Noland, or to Louis's Unfurleds or Stripes. The latter kind of color picture

76. *First One*. 1964. Water-miscible acrylic on canvas,
92 1/2 × 69 1/2". Collection Mr. and Mrs. Frank H. Porter, Chagrin Falls, Ohio

first emerged fully in the work of Matisse and the Fauves, but the initial impetus had come from Van Gogh, Gauguin, and Cézanne. Cézanne had systematized color intensities as a way of restoring value accents, light and dark accents, while continuing to employ Impressionist color and light. The Fauves abstracted his system still further in an effort to heighten the impact of color. Instead of dividing a surface into planes of color, they made a single hue stand for the whole local color of an object.

The Fauve kind of picture creates a color effect of contrast by juxtaposing pure, discrete, and clearly separated hues. Sharp differences in the value of hues at full intensity—for example, blue and yellow—are accepted for the vigor and optical energy their contrasts evoke. Far brighter and more obviously colorful than the paintings of the Impressionists, the Fauve pictures stress declarative immediacy and the individual identity of each hue. White is often used to heighten and help unify an optical dazzle; and light seems to be reflected by the picture rather than, as with Impressionism, located within it. Such pictures live by vivid, ringing complementaries or by unexpected juxtapositions. Matisse and, among abstract painters, Kenneth Noland have been masters of this type of color invention.

Unity is one problem in this kind of picture: keeping the separate hues from canceling each other out and creating an effect the Germans call *bunt*. The most frequent solutions—evident in the work of Matisse as well as in the stained paintings of Louis, Noland, and Olitski—have been to give clear dominance to one color in terms of area size, or to resort to a generous use of white.[12]

Another problem involves the clear edges and emphatic designs that are created by juxtaposing areas of intense color. Primacy of color can only be maintained by preventing the design from taking on an inert, filled-in look, from seeming

77. *"Ausstellung Signale,"* exhibition at the Kunsthalle, Basel, Switzerland, 1965. Left to right: *One Time,* 1964; *Green Jazz,* 1962; *Chemise,* 1963

78. *One Time.* 1964.
Oil-miscible acrylic on canvas, 82 × 69 1/4".
Collection of the artist

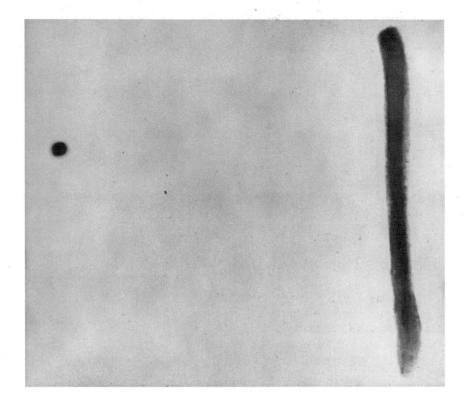

79. *Butterfly Kiss*. 1964.
Oil-miscible acrylic on canvas, 68 × 78".
Collection of the artist

80. *Big Diagonal*. 1965.
Oil-miscible acrylic on canvas, 117 × 93". Collection of the artist

merely poster-like and graphic. Also, since the eye first grasps differences of light and dark, the picture must be organized so that the sharp value changes from one color to the next do not cancel out or compete with the force of color as hue and intensity. Noland and Louis often solved these problems by resorting to various kinds of symmetry, which more or less obviate compositional decisions after a certain point.

Olitski's spray technique tends toward a different kind of color picture, one which might be called "impressionist," although there are much earlier precedents, especially in seventeenth- and eighteenth-century painting. Here the interest is primarily in a color experience that results from the subtle modulation of color into color across the surface. Anything that interrupts the continuous movement of color—sharp changes of hue and value, as well as drawing—is de-emphasized. Usually some method of painterly application—such as the impressionist touch, Louis's layerings, or Olitski's spray—produces this flow of color.

The impressionist picture tends toward density and warmth, middle grayness and an initial monochromatic look; coloristic richness emerges only gradually. Overall tonality dominates, and changes of hue emerge as fugitive, suggestive, evanescent, and nuanced. Owing to the radically reduced value range, slight color shifts appear as identical with equally slight value shifts. The emphasis is not on the identity of individual hues, but on a single, richly varied chromatic substance informed by an absorbent inner light.

Since the impressionist-type color picture develops primarily *across* the surface, the artist is not forced to continually step back to balance out his composition, as is often the case with the Fauve-type painter. His main difficulties have to do with accentuation and variety, the introduction of sharp, pungent changes of hue and/or value. A secondary problem concerns stopping the flow and turning the field into a picture.

81. *Judith Juice*. 1965.
Water-miscible acrylic on canvas, 98 × 68″. Kasmin, Ltd., London, England

82. *Pink Shush*. 1965. Water-miscible acrylic on canvas, 79 × 66''. Private collection

Motifs from nature helped the Impressionists to achieve accentuation and pictorial completeness.[13] Olitski, as an abstract painter, looked to his manner of application and his recognition of the differences between the margins of a flat, more or less uniformly accented abstract picture and its center. So, for example, with a few marks or strokes at the edges, he has been able to introduce what are often abrupt, Fauve-like bursts of hue and value while simultaneously declaring his fields as self-contained pictorial units.[14]

For Olitski, spraying was a means of creating a new surface as well as color fusion. All modernist pictures since Cubism are oriented to flatness as their principle of unity; their success depends first of all, if not finally, on a felt continuity between the illusion and the resistant plane surface.[15] Expressively, this conveys a taut immediacy, a withheld directness, which modernist sensibility finds especially exhilarating. After the phases of collage and Synthetic Cubism, this sense for flatness slackened. As part of a general loosening up and separation of figure and ground, painters were content with a more ideal picture plane. But as the literal materials of painting have increasingly taken on a more exclusive role in the final effect, flatness has again reasserted itself. As we have already seen, there has been a tendency since World War II toward ways of working and paint applications that in and of themselves create flatness through the continuous tactility of the whole surface. At the same time, this flatness must be visually alive.

A related factor has been the emphasis on color during this same period. If the new flatness makes a strong tactile appeal, pure color aims at an exclusively optical one. A central problem for the abstract color painter, then, especially when working with broad color fields, is to somehow unite optical illusion and tactile surface; to render them continuous. Obviously, this cannot occur without compromise and the subordination of one or the other. The solution, especially when the color field

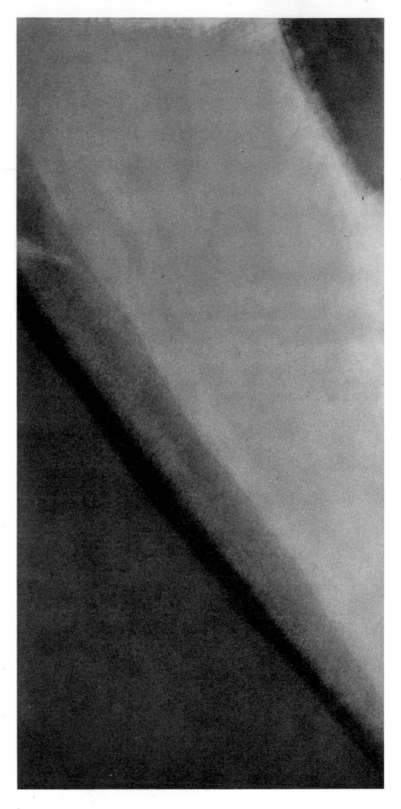

83. *Lovely Doukhabor*. 1965.
Water-miscible acrylic on canvas, 96 × 40".
Whereabouts unknown

84. *Ishtar Melted*. 1965.
Water-miscible acrylic on canvas, 61 × 21".
The Art Museum, Princeton University, Princeton, N.J.
Gift of Steven Schapiro and Anthony Zerbe

is broad and uninterrupted, lies primarily with paint consistency and application.[16] Staining, by identifying disembodied optical color with the weave of the canvas fabric, automatically re-creates the new modernist flatness. And painters working with stain, like Noland, Dzubas, and the early Olitski, have often strengthened this inherent property of their technique by leaving areas of bare canvas, making explicit the identity of color and canvas texture. (To further strengthen tactility, stain painters have sometimes teased and scumbled their surfaces to get a rich, velvety or suedelike texture, or mixed agents such as pearlessence into their pigments.) When completely covered with color, the canvas weave becomes less a factor in the final effect. In Olitski's paintings of 1964, a single hue threatens to cover the entire surface. To give a sense of expansion and internal delimitedness and to underscore the identification of color and canvas, he left areas of raw canvas at the margins. These edges in turn affected the character of the field. As Olitski later wrote, "Edge is drawing and drawing is always *on* the surface. The color areas take on the appearance of overlay, and if the conception of form is governed by edge—no matter how successfully it possesses the surface—paint, even when stained into raw canvas, remains on or above the surface. I think, on the contrary, of color being *in*, not *on*, the surface."[17]

Sprayed color, then, meant a new kind of tactility that did not depend on edge. As Clement Greenberg has observed, "The grainy surface Olitski creates with his way of spraying is a new kind of paint surface. It offers tactile associations hitherto foreign, more or less, to picture-making; and it does new things with color. Together with color, it contrives an illusion of depth back to the picture's surface; it is as if that surface, in all its literalness, were enlarged to contain a world of color and light differentiations impossible to flatness but which yet manages not to violate flatness."[18]

85. *New Time*. 1965.
Water-miscible acrylic on canvas,
106 × 23″. Collection Alkis P. Klonaridis

86. *Jump*. 1965.
Water-miscible acrylic on canvas, 92 3/4 × 32".
Collection Mr. and Mrs. David Mirvish, Toronto, Ont.

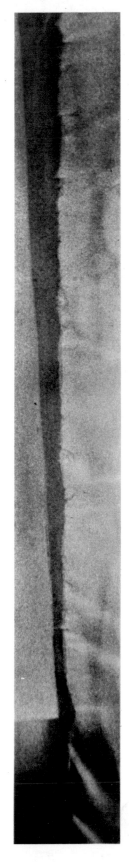

87. *Free*. 1966.
Water-miscible acrylic on canvas, 118 × 15''.
Collection of the artist

One might say that the sculptural appeal Olitski had eliminated in the form of contour drawing now reasserted itself as
a varied tactile surface. So, too, it asserted itself as light and
dark, as shading, but a shading not attached to an edge or
plane but identical with the thickness and thinness of the paint
(as with Louis's Veils). By spraying paint unevenly, Olitski
achieved different paint densities, which automatically result
in different color intensities as well as in light and dark shifts;
and again, thanks to spraying, these shifts can be very finely
graded.[19] In this way, Olitski reintroduced traditional chiaroscuro, with all its associations of richness and mystery, into the
abstract picture. (It had not received this much emphasis since
Analytical Cubism.) The color plus the chiaroscuro in these
pictures can be deceptively gorgeous and ingratiating. Like
Monet before him, Olitski sometimes appears to be testing the
modernist tolerance for sheer lusciousness. But these lovely
hues and softly suggestive depths are stiffened to the resistant
surface. An indulgent sensuousness of French painting and
Rembrandtesque romanticism are tautened and withheld,
transformed into something impassive, even grand.

Early spray pictures like *Rexus* have a wonderful fragility
and sensuousness without softness; the spray clings to the
surface like a fine dust.[20] Sometimes a margin of raw canvas is
left at the edge so that the paint covering becomes, at that
point, a thin liquid film. These pictures seem to fulfill Olitski's
own stated wish for color with no support at all, as if color had
been sprayed into the air and had remained there or at least
had been caught there by the canvas surface itself.[21]

But the delicate surfaces of the early spray paintings can
also be seen as calling for increased flatness because of the
more sensible illusion which spraying evokes. So, too, the
fine-grained effect of spray imposes a certain kind of scale—a
certain feeling of depiction—on these pictures which makes
their delicacy seem somewhat remote, compared, at least, to

Olitski's later work. In 1967, he began to reaffirm a stronger sense of flatness by freighting his pigment with various elements such as gel or other plastic agents so as to render them more viscous, hence more coarsely or broadly tactile (or reflective).

The last of the stain paintings, such as *Lovely Doukhabor,* 1965 (pl. 83) as well as some of the early spray paintings, such as *Kusha,* 1965, show complementary color changes and are not very successful. The same is true of the paintings in Olitski's first show of spray pictures at Poindexter Gallery in 1965, most of which have prismatic colors, marked contrasts of hue near the middle of the picture, and a soft, luminous, but non-specific depth. Gradually Olitski discovered that the real advantage of spray was not, as he first thought, in permitting him to change hue within the field, but in the possibility of altering the density of paint and therefore the color and value modulation without interrupting the continuity of the surface. Already in 1966 he began concentrating more on light and dark within a single color. A full intensity hue was taken either at the light end of the scale and then graded into a darker shade (*Heavy Gold*), or at the dark end of the scale and graded into a tint (*Galiloo,* pl. 94, or *Prince Patutsky's Command*). Occasionally he would try to achieve a sharp hue change—even a complementary change—by valuing the two colors very closely (*Thigh Smoke,* pl. 89), but more often than not this misfired, and as 1966 wore on Olitski settled more and more for a general monochromatic field.

By the end of 1968 and in early 1969, Olitski came to see that his concept had more to do with painting and paint than with color per se (unlike Noland, whose approach is exactly the opposite). His surfaces became more palpable, his monochromes less prismatic; neutrals increasingly predominated. (The stress on material or tactile continuity of the field meant that prismatic color could create an oversaturated feeling.) Increas-

88. *Implications*. 1966.
Water-miscible acrylic on canvas, 116 × 48".
Collection Dr. and Mrs. Arthur L. Prensky, St. Louis, Mo.

89. *Thigh Smoke*. 1966. Water-miscible acrylic on canvas, 167 × 98 1/2''.
Seattle-First National Bank, Corporate Art Collection, Seattle, Wash.

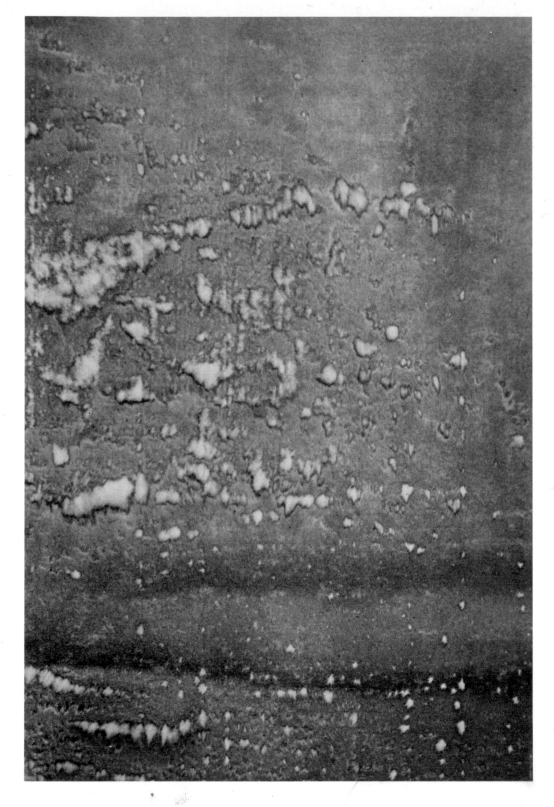

90. *Loose Bottom*. 1966.
Water-miscible acrylic on canvas, 45 × 74".
Private collection

ingly he invested in fresh and different ways of working. The margins became very aggressive in 1966 and 1967 (*Julius and His Friends*, pl. 96; *High A Yellow*). But again the logic of his concept asserted itself, a logic which demands emphasis on the continuity of the surface. At the end of 1968 and into early 1969, texture changes became even more marked. Paint congeals on the surface in the most tactile way and value change is more and more literally identified with a change of paint covering. Contrasts between matte and shiny became more important in 1970, but a bigger change occurred in 1972, when he began using heavy gel and a squeegee,[22] with which he was able to achieve a one-to-one visual identity between a paint density change and value change. The pictures became transparent but also literal and physical in the scale of their incident and in the sensible density of their buildup. Unlike the early spray pictures, where a disembodied, impersonal pictorial substance seems caught on the surface, here the canvas is simply covered with paint. Like all great solutions in art—one thinks of Monet's waterlilies or Mondrian's classic phase—Olitski's is the most simple, natural, straightforward, and flexible solution imaginable at this historic moment. Today abstract painting is so *there*, so literally flat or literal in its flatness, that even the edge-controlled linearism of Mondrian seems too depicted. At the same time, the new abstract painting demands large scale and allows color possibilities that were closed to Mondrian and his contemporaries. If Mondrian drew the logical conclusion from Cubism, then Olitski has done the same thing for postwar abstraction. Mondrian's great innovation was to conceive of painting simply as the *division of the surface*, while Olitski's is to conceive of painting simply as the *covering of the surface* with paint. In both cases, the logical conclusion is the simplest one and therefore the most definitive (but also the most difficult to appreciate as something inspired and achieved).

91. *Maximum*. 1966. Water-miscible acrylic on canvas, 86 1/2 × 157". Collection Mr. and Mrs. Charles Gilman, Jr., New York

92. *Beyond Bounds*. 1966. Water-miscible acrylic on canvas, 92 1/4 × 62''.
The Wellesley College Museum, Wellesley, Mass.

From another point of view, Olitski brings to fruition ideas first proposed by the Abstract Expressionists. The so-called painterly wing of Abstract Expressionists, and especially Willem de Kooning, discovered that the mixing and muddying of colors on the surface produces effects of light and dark, and therefore shading. But this only worked for De Kooning when he had control of an object (usually a figure) and never for the space *around* the object, which becomes "mere" filler. De Kooning's abstract paintings are even more problematic. The broad free strokes he needs for big scale deny him control of the space, and his many prismatic colors fight the unity of the sculptural surface. Olitski eschews prismatic colors and his basic unit is the surface, not the stroke. In this way, he fully exploits the Abstract Expressionist's discovery that different paint densities and fusings yield a "natural" chiaroscuro and color.

For their part, the abstract color wing of Abstract Expressionism—notably Newman and Rothko—invented simple, large, continuous areas of color, but lacked Pollock's and De Kooning's physical, direct sense of surface. It was Olitski's reformulation of the latter that permitted him to exploit the former. In the end, Olitski, like Kenneth Noland, has accomplished what the Abstract Expressionist pioneers grasped only tenuously: the creation of an abstract picture as an autonomous, spiritual object made solely from painting's own irreducible materials of paint and canvas and from their concomitant expressive features of scale, surface, and color. "Fulfillment" here has a lot to do with emphasizing the *abstract* implications of Abstract Expressionism.[23] This in turn has permitted fulfillment in terms of sheer prolificness as well as range of expressiveness. In both categories, Noland and Olitski far outdistance the pioneers. Indeed, one could go on to say that Olitski fulfills Kandinsky's notion of an abstract painterly art while Noland

93. *Doulma*. 1966. Water-miscible acrylic on canvas, 68 1/2 × 90″. Collection Mr. and Mrs. David Mirvish, Toronto, Ont.

fulfills Mondrian's notion of an abstract geometric one, so that subsequent abstraction would seem to have to locate itself somewhere between them. But I don't want to leave the impression that these two painters are *only* a fulfillment. Their own unique contributions are already clear enough. One could characterize them by saying that Noland challenges the density and weight of traditional easel painting, making it expressively weightless, while Olitski challenges its drama. (See Chapter 2.)

In art, the revision of one crucial variable implies an alteration of all the rest. A heavy, thick buildup of paint on the surface means literal density and opacity. It asks for its own kind of illusion of transparency and depth. Characteristically, Olitski accomplished this by using, in addition to spraying, devices he had learned in art schools and museums: blendings, scumbling, glazes, impasto, and varnish—painting as the old masters understood it, a complicated, layered buildup of the actual depth of the surface in order to induce imaginative pictorial depths. Real opacity and transparency are asked to be elusive, suggestive. Expressive emphasis falls on relations of thick to thin, transparent to opaque, matte to shiny, and on the distinctive configuration determined by the means of application. With these techniques Olitski again repossesses a distinctive aspect of traditional painting culture,[24] as he did with the rich chiaroscuro created by spraying. (Olitski himself refers to spraying as "only one special case within the medium of glazing.") Given the buildup and monochrome, the application acts something like drawing, making another kind of drawing—at the edges—become less crucial compositionally. The inside is more plastic, less uniform, but no less homogeneous. So now the literalness of the outside edge is less felt as limiting or even delimiting.[25]

If the increased tactility of his flattened, continuous surfaces is a result of Olitski's efforts to give a more taut unity to his color fields, it is also the result of a very personal artistic pref-

94. *Galliloo*. 1967.
Water-miscible acrylic on canvas, 93 1/2 × 43″.
Collection of the artist

95. *Blue Bonzer*. 1967. Water-miscible acrylic on canvas, 34 1/2 × 144''. Private collection, Malibu, Calif.

96. *Julius and Friends*. 1967.
Water-miscible acrylic on canvas,
71 1/2 × 149 3/4".
Private collection, Boston, Mass.

erence. Unlike Noland, who seeks to escape the sculptural through expressive weightlessness, Olitski, as we have already noted, always seeks to retain something of the plastic fullness, the sculptural character of older painting. So his most radical innovations are often in the service of tradition, efforts to salvage for modernism the richness of the past. The result is an extraordinary range of textural effects: caked, encrusted, hard and shiny, waxy, gritty, crumbly, grainy, milky, and ceramic-like.[26] These surfaces both seduce and distance the viewer, combining the sensual delights and beauties of belle peinture with the taut impassiveness which belongs to the best of abstract painting: extreme sensitivity merged with deadpan restraint. Initial simplicity, even blankness, ultimately yields richness and fullness of experience.[27] The viewer's reactions are compressed within a radically narrowed range, challenging him to see with greater aesthetic acuteness.[28] Wisps and blushes of color and shading are always on the verge of congealing into a legible pattern, but before this can quite occur, the flux and shifting begins again. The not-quite-graspable character, the suggestiveness and ambiguity, is of a piece with those rare and fugitive hues that emerge only after sustained looking. His work challenges the viewer without asking to be liked and it rewards concentration with a justified sensual fullness and beauty.[29]

Extreme asymmetry of design and occult balance, highly refined nuanced effects issuing from a pregnant "emptiness," these are qualities known from Far Eastern art, the product of a highly sophisticated and self-conscious artistic culture like our own. But in their painterly directness and amplitude, in their non-decorative involution and drama, in their self-sufficiency, Olitski's paintings remain very much part of the Western easel tradition, although they hold a very special place at the extreme limits of this tradition.

97. *Central Heating*. 1967. Water-miscible acrylic on canvas, 79 1/4 × 197 1/2″. Collection Mr. and Mrs. David Mirvish, Toronto, Ont.

NOTES TO CHAPTER ONE

1. Letter from Olitski to the author, June 21, 1980.

2. See Lawrence Alloway in the catalogue *Matter Painting*, London, Institute of Contemporary Art, 1960.

3. Letter from Olitski, op. cit.

4. One of the best writers on Olitski, Charles Millard, plays down the relationship between French postwar abstraction and Olitski's impasto paintings. For example, Millard points out that Fautrier, while producing works that resemble Olitski's impastos, is essentially working with a different sensibility: that of a "miniaturist interested in the careful manipulation of small scale form and the precise working of surfaces." Instead, Millard sees Olitski's impasto pictures in the context of contemporary Spanish painters like Tàpies and, especially, Luis Feito. According to Millard, they were "much exhibited" in New York in these years (see Charles Millard, "Jules Olitski," *Hudson Review*, Oct. 1974, pp. 401–408). I have been unable to find any exhibitions of Feito's work in New York before 1960. Moreover, the work of these two artists, Olitski and Feito, looks more alike in black and white reproduction than in the original. A connection is certainly possible, but in my view not likely. With Feito, everything is obvious and confected, and based almost completely on black and white rather than a neutral range. Also, his gritty, sooty surfaces are very unlike Olitski's.

I myself have wanted to see the influence of Fautrier in the impasto pictures, but it may be that despite a certain visual similarity no influence really exists. Olitski doesn't remember seeing works by Fautrier until after he did his matter paintings (letter from Olitski, op. cit.). It should also be remembered that the impasto paintings were begun in the United States five years after Olitski returned from Europe.

5. Letter from Olitski, op. cit.

6. *Ten O'Clock* (pl. 39), *Sacrifice of Isaac, Lucy's Desire, Lucy Lubric* (pl. 38), *Empress Theresa*, all from late 1959 or early 1960. Also, a picture like *Osculum Silence*, 1960 (pl. 47), from a bit later, marks a transition from thick to thin surfaces.

7. In the earliest dye pictures, like *Potsy* (pl. 50) or *The Blush* (pl. 46), both 1960, it is as if Olitski is using harsh value oppositions and vivid, biting contours to create the effect of a hole in the surface or to make the inscribed area seem to jump or push off the surface: in other words, to get effects which old master painters explicitly avoided as detrimental to their illusion, but which an abstract painter like Olitski exploits for directness. As noted, these effects were like abstractions of the aggressive impasto areas and glowing colors of the previous series. Staining and the presiding unifying effect of the raw canvas surface (especially when areas are left unpainted) gave coherence to these effects. Raw canvas meant that the most vibrating, "popping" edges could be set against each other and yet both could be read ultimately on the same spatial level. The raw canvas area between also became equally charged and alive. This effect is enhanced by primary colors which pull away from—that is, contrast with—each other. So Olitski gave up the unusual colors (as well as black) that he used between 1960 and 1962 and in 1963 began to stress primaries and raw canvas.

8. For an excellent discussion of these paintings, see Michael Fried, "New York Letter," *Art International*, Mar. 1964, pp. 40–42.

9. On this point, consult Michael Fried, op. cit.

10. All the major painters of recent years have learned to escape the feeling of the framing edge so as to get a feeling of expansion or "openness" that seems to be part of our period style. That this openness is crucial is proved in a negative way by the dead inertia that infects most shaped canvases, that is, where edge is stressed more than the inside.

The marginings, which occur already in 1964, assert themselves over the actual edge, like Newman's "zips" and Mondrian's lines, to further reduce its force, to cancel or neutralize its enclosing potential, to open up and unbalance the picture *as a whole* (something that began with Mondrian).

11. It is interesting that red is such a crucial color for both the falling curtain pictures and the field pictures. Not only is it by far the predominant color used for the field, but most of the best of these pictures are red: *Flaming On, Flaubert Red* (pl. 73), *Inside Voyage, Zem Zem, Deep Drag, Prince Patutsky's Gamble, The A-6*. This is all the more surprising when one thinks that Olitski has hardly ever been successful with red since 1965. On the other

hand, he doesn't try it all that often anymore. Like any true colorist, Olitski lets the development of materials lead him, through trial and error, to new areas of color. He wants always to rediscover his color sensibility. He doesn't want an a priori notion of it, just as he doesn't want an a priori notion of surface. Like Noland, he is programmatic about keeping his art unprogrammed—open, developing. (See my *Kenneth Noland*, New York, Harry N. Abrams, 1977.)

12. An alternate solution is, of course, to close-value the whole picture as Noland has often done.

It is interesting to note that Matisse and the Fauves also followed Cézanne in leaving exposed relatively large primed and sized areas of white canvas. Morris Louis's Unfurleds are a classic example of this type of "Fauve" solution.

13. By painting in close values and by creating an equalized surface tension, with every square inch receiving the same emphasis, the Impressionists automatically achieved a very cohesive unity. Hence, they were not interested in composition per se or in its formal elaboration; they gave attention to tonal recession but not to compositional accents. They did not really compose but chose scenes that composed themselves, that gave a merely sufficient sense of completeness, such as a centered road or a view that mirrors itself in the reflecting surface of water.

On the question of the relation between accentuation and nature in the Impressionist picture, see Clement Greenberg, "The Late Monet," in *Art and Culture*, Boston, Beacon Press, 1961, pp. 37–45. As Greenberg has pointed out in regard to the reception of Monet's work, "What is missed is geometrical, diagrammatic, and sculptural structure; in its stead, the Impressionists achieved structure by accentuation and modulation of points and areas of color and value, a kind of composition which is not inherently less 'structural' than the other kind" (p. 51). This applies equally to Olitski. It is also worth noting that the charges of being "too pretty" and "merely sensuous," or alternately, too much the result of theory (the critics of Impressionism meant the theory of optics) have been the main objections to both Monet and Olitski.

Several writers have wanted to see a relation between Olitski's spraying and Neo-Impressionism. Within the terms of the model used above, Neo-Impressionism is just one form of the Impressionist-type picture. More specifically, however, it is also true that with its regularized, tiny dots which facilitate and control the blending of colors and the transitions of value as color, Neo-Impressionist technique bears a close relationship to Olitski's spraying. Both approaches inherently exclude sharp contours, which Seurat, as long as he wanted to focus on near objects, had to add almost as a second operation, as the silhouette. For this reason, there often is something willful about the contour drawing in his pictures from the middle 1880s, a willfulness that becomes stylization in the later '80s. Perhaps this was the main reason why he turned so often to smaller pictures and landscapes (far vision) at this time.

14. These edges also act to shape or inflect the surface, to open or close it laterally, to flatten it, to give it depth (by overlapping it) or forward thrust (by being overlapped by it), or to push it out at one point and pin it down or blend it back at another. It can make the surface seem to angle off, or ripple, or billow, or seem to be pulled tight, or hang loose. Originally the main intention may have been to overcome a set, balanced, static effect of the all-over monochrome field (as seen, say, in *Tin Lizzy Green*), but once discovered, Olitski has exploited these marginings or salvagings in many different ways.

15. It has been one of Clement Greenberg's main contributions to the interpretation of modern art that he has harped on this point. See, for example, his "Collages," in *Art and Culture*, pp. 70–83. It is also probably necessary to add that he has always denied that flatness in itself is either good or bad.

16. This point was only imperfectly grasped by Barnett Newman, who flattened his color fields with vertical bands. These establish the picture plane all right, but the rectilinear design does not directly affect the field; it merely implies flatness by frontality, by referring the interior to the shape of the support. Newman's fields are sometimes ambivalent and usually unemphatic in their flatness, for the illusion and the surface—the bands—are not explicitly continuous (unless, of course, the value and color are exactly right). One possibility that Newman temporarily explored was uniform, opaque, unyielding color, but this made his pictures seem brittle and sometimes even graphic. The main obstacle to solving this problem was Newman's relative disinterest in paint quality.

Of the colorists of the first generation, Olitski might be seen as closest to Rothko. Both create suspended, impressionistic color masses that suggest atmosphere and light. But besides Olitski's far greater range as a colorist, he differs from Rothko in being much more "positivistic"— that is, direct, immediate, and literal—whether in his stained work or in his spray paintings. Rothko's pictures are more traditionally "inside"—both inside the rectangle and farther back in pictorial space. Like Newman, Rothko relied as much on drawing and frontality as on paint surface per se to affirm the picture plane. Expressively, Rothko's paintings have a confrontational drama, while Olitski's are more physical yet paradoxically "turn their back" on the viewer, offering him almost nothing at all to hang on to in terms of design.

17. Jules Olitski, "Painting in Color," in *XXXIII International Biennial Exhibition of Art*, Venice, 1966, p. 39.

18. Clement Greenberg, "Jules Olitski," in *XXXIII International Biennial Exhibition of Art*, p. 38. This grainy texture is the result of the combination of air and paint produced by a spray gun. If the canvas is unprimed, the air pressure blows up nap from the bare surface, which also counts in the final result. By varying the gun's distance from the canvas and the fineness of the burst, the artist can further alter this surface texture, density, color saturation, etc.

19. For a history of the use of spraying in painting, see Paul C. Mills' introduction to the catalogue of the exhibition *Spray*, presented by the Santa Barbara Museum of Art in 1971. Mills points out that spray and stenciling were used in cave painting and that the spray look appears in Western painting already in the work of Toulouse-Lautrec. Spray was used by Man Ray from 1917 to 1919 for his "aerographs" and was often used at the Bauhaus by Kandinsky and Klee (pl. 3), among others.

David Smith used spray in paintings done in the late 1950s. They were shown at French & Co. in 1959 and were seen by Olitski, but he didn't like them. According to Thomas B. Hess, Barnett Newman was the first American painter to try using spray. In 1949–52 he experimented with a spray, but found it more trouble than it was worth, so went back to painting by hand, with a brush (*Barnett Newman*, New York, Walker and Co., 1969, p. 44). *Cathedra* of 1951, an eight-by-eighteen-foot blue painting, was one of the resulting works.

20. As Rosalind Krauss has noted, the drawn lines and especially the masked-off edges of different value (which might be seen as a throwback to the idea behind the drawing-board pictures) can cause the interiors of these pictures to seem to slant back obliquely in a series of "foreshortened movements" that peel off, as it were, from the painting's frontality. (Rosalind Krauss, "On Frontality," *Artforum*, May 1968, pp. 40–46.) This was one way to avoid the stasis and containment that were dangers in the early spray pictures due to the dominance of the (given) rectangular shape of the picture. So, too, the color mists come and go, here congealing into intensity of hue and opaqueness, there disappearing into wafts of transparency. As with Pollock, Olitski's all-overness must allow for movement together with main and secondary centers of interest—inflection—but these are now secondary and the perception of them demands intense looking. The first effect may be that everything is the same. On these pictures, and Olitski's work of the late 1960s, see Darby Bannard, "Quality, Style, and Olitski," *Artforum*, Oct. 1972, esp. p. 67.

21. See Chronology entry for 1964, p. 207 of this volume.

22. While in general the pictures get coarser after 1973, Olitski always does more refined, smoother pictures too, usually at the same time. His range in any one year is enormous, making it often difficult to date his pictures.

23. See my *Kenneth Noland*, op. cit., especially Chapter 3.

24. Here is E. A. Carmean describing the process involved in *Hyksos Factor III* of 1975 (pl. 121):

"In *Hyksos Factor III* . . . there were four separate steps. Initially, the canvas was covered with a grey color, rolled onto the surface so as to leave a rough, allover texture. This ground was then modeled in certain areas by using transparent medium (without color) which acts like a glaze to strengthen and modify the grey surface. Next Olitski applied a mixture of black pigment in medium which . . . when squeezed across the surface separates into strokes of light and dark. Actually this layer is composed of black paint making a third surface, while transparent areas further glaze the initial level. Finally, over this another level of transparent medium is squeezed on, transforming the black strokes. The result is that the planes are suspended, in part, above the grey ground, which glows through them. These planes in turn shift in and out through the final surface glaze." [E. A. Carmean, "Olitski, Cubism, and Transparency," *Arts,* Nov. 1975, pp. 53–57.]

25. Most of Olitski's post-1965 pictures have been verticals and most of them are high in key. In fact, most color painting since Impressionism is high in key. One reason is that the eye has an easier time making fine discriminations at the light end of the scale than it does at the dark end. So more variation is possible. Secondly, the light end of the scale makes the tactility of the surface texture more visible (think for example of the difference in this respect between the black and the white areas in a Mondrian painting—or in Rembrandt's for that matter). So lightness can help reinforce flatness.

As to shape of the format, Olitski did several tall, thin pictures like *Unlocked* in 1966, but he has also done long, narrow ones (like *Scroncher,* 18 5/8 by 214 1/4"). In *Unlocked,* the interior masked "edge" divides the narrow surface. Noland has painted pictures in which a few narrow stripes are the whole picture; Newman, ones in which his "zip" is the whole picture. In each case, it is a question of the artist pushing his own created conventions as far as they can go, or turning them on their heads. It is a kind of play, but a serious play that is always pushing for an opening; for new creative possibilities.

In 1974, Olitski introduced the novelty of dividing the picture down the center with one or two lines (or "edges"). This is what he had tried

in *Unlocked,* but now he did it in large, broad pictures. This feature is more in the nature of an enrichment and elaboration of Olitski's concept than a new departure.

26. Olitski uses an enormous variety of techniques in applying paint: hand, mitten, roller, broom, mop, etc. He also employs various methods to remove it: scrapers, knives, etc. Occasionally he has varied his support, working on ceramic and carpet surfaces (1968).

27. For an insightful discussion of how some of Olitski's pictures work, see Ken Carpenter, "On Order in the Paintings of Jules Olitski," *Art International,* Dec. 1972, pp. 26–30.

28. So narrow is the range that it is almost impossible to distinguish between real shadows caused by relief on the surface, the implied shadows resulting from different paint densities, and, finally, the actual shadows caused by uneven lighting in the place where the picture hangs.

29. The female nude occurs again and again in Olitski's work—in the scatalogical blindfold paintings, in certain of the impastos, and in the swelling curves and breast- or nipple-like shapes which were taken from photographs of the female nude and used in the 1960–63 pictures. Olitski also used an old postcard of a reclining female nude seen from behind as the starting point for his "Nathalie Type" series (pl. 131) done in mid-1976. The female nude is also the main subject of Olitski's drawings (pls. 139–42). Everywhere Olitski's art relates to tradition and the old masters just as it always betrays an enormous sensuality.

98. Olitski in his New Hampshire studio. 1980

TWO OLITSKI'S PAINTING AND MODERNISM

Attending to a picture aesthetically, that even distribution of detached attention by means of which the viewer savors the wholeness and unity of a painting, is a matter of suspending practical seeing, the world of objects, in favor of the surface. It represents an alteration of normal, purposive looking by letting the visual field itself structure what is seen. Vision is spread equally and thus tends toward the flat and the optical with the areas between objects becoming as important as the objects themselves. From time immemorial every painter must have taken up this mental attitude by narrowing his eyes or stepping back from his work when he wished to assess the overall distribution of visual weights.

Impressionism, which was a dissolving of naturalism into aestheticism, revolutionized painting by assuming this attitude *toward nature*; that is to say, the Impressionists sought—insofar as it was possible—an identification of the visual field and the pictorial surface.[1] Hence their interest in optical color. The attempt was made to see everything as if the eye were equidistant from it (the so-called "far vision"). By eliminating underpainting and glazes and by using conspicuous but neutralized brushstrokes, each of approximately the same size and shape, they got a very homogeneous and therefore discrete surface, one which gave an unprecedented importance to the material of paint and which permitted them to work across the surface without stepping back as often as was necessary with older painting.

Undermining this, however, was perspective and the structure of reality. By isolating the visual field as a whole the Impressionists had made surface and depth, at least potentially, discontinuous. Even in Monet's paintings of lily pads, a motif which was chosen primarily because it easily aligned itself with the surface, the identification remains incomplete since Monet still had to deal with a foreground and a background,

99. *Doessy*. 1967.
Water-miscible acrylic on canvas,
51 3/4 × 19 3/4".
Collection Dr. and Mrs. Henry L. Foster,
Newton Center, Mass.

100. *Free and Fast*. 1968.
Water-miscible acrylic on canvas, 110 × 50".
Washington University Gallery of Art, St. Louis, Mo.

101. Piet Mondrian. *Pier and Ocean*. 1914.
Charcoal and white watercolor on buff paper, 34 5/8
× 44". Oval composition, 33 × 40".
The Museum of Modern Art, New York.
Mrs. Simon Guggenheim Fund

102. Piet Mondrian. *Composition*. 1927.
Oil on canvas, 15 1/2 × 20".
Collection Drs. Harold and Alice Ladas, New York

each of which asked for a different kind of articulation.[2] The visual and pictorial fields were always to remain in conflict so long as the structure of reality had to be accommodated; the breaking of this structure in favor of the surface was, of course, the task of Cubism.

Fauvism eliminated Impressionist evenness in favor of a hierarchy of accents—the traditional stepping back and balancing out. From this point of view Fauvism was conservative, but the problem it raised, that of avoiding decoration by relating flattened forms across a flattened surface, eventually drove the Cubists to their radical step of subverting perspective and the autonomy of objects; nature was no longer chosen for the sake of two-dimensionality but was adapted to it. The essential means to achieve such an adaptation was rectilinear drawing and *passage*, the dissociation of contour from interior shading.

Seeking the directness and explicitness of sharp edges, Mondrian dispensed with *passage* and gave full expressive weight to rectilinear drawing. And almost immediately he drove his pictures toward an all-over evenness of accent in his so-called "plus-and-minus" pictures of 1914–17 (pl. 101). Then Mondrian drew back. For the results were for the most part more assertions than realizations, more statements about pictorial logic than major pictures. And given his self-imposed restriction to horizontal and vertical lines, all-overness threatened Mondrian's continued development as a painter.

To recover the possibility of variation he reverted to traditional dominance and subordination, dramatic imbalance—or, as he called it, "dramatic equilibrium." Giving up all-overness, he retained its holistic effect. By 1920 Mondrian's surface was divided by crisp lines which exactly repeated the edges of the rectangle (pl. 102); all was woven together and the picture's singleness was forced upon the viewer in a new way. Together with the extremely flat, even assertiveness of the surface, this

103. *Hold and Roll*. 1968. Water-miscible acrylic on canvas, 67 × 162″. Kasmin, Ltd., London, England

104. *Instant Loveland*. 1968. Water-miscible acrylic on canvas, 120 × 252″. Kasmin, Ltd., London, England

105. *4th Hope*. 1969. Water-miscible acrylic on canvas, 5 × 97″. Collection of the artist

106. *Rug Painting, No. 2*. 1969.
Water-miscible acrylic on rug mounted on plywood, 55 × 28 1/4".
Collection of the artist

resulted in a kind of wholeness. Rather than shapes being balanced out within a fictive depth, the picture balanced itself out.

Contrary to Mondrian, Miró and Klee exaggerated *passage* by relegating line to foreground and shading to background in an effort to free their drawing from the demands of strict rectilinearity and achieve a looser, more open feeling. In their pictures automatic graphic effects float on or in an indeterminate atmosphere or field evoked by softly shaded color areas tinted or soaked into the surface. As we have noted, Barnett Newman and Mark Rothko began with this Surrealist version of late Cubism; they eliminated the over-writing and were left with luminous and potentially penetrable and shimmering fields which they then stiffened and flattened with simplified rectilinear design.

Olitski, too, had Miró in mind, especially after 1960. Sometimes he would do canvases which contained only a few small dots or disks of color eccentrically positioned in a raw canvas field. These were painted at the same time as such pictures as *Flaubert Red* (pl. 73), which show positively colored fields; and Olitski has said that what interested him most in Miró's work (pl. 2) at this time were the *backgrounds* of his pictures.[3] Without the over-writing, Miró's backgrounds became foreground, or rather the distinction between background and foreground was abolished in favor of the distinction between field and edge; the picture became an all-over continuity of light and color.

In arriving at the all-over picture, Olitski had the dramatic precedent of Jackson Pollock's work (pl. 23). By the mid-1940s Pollock had also arrived at the Surrealist type of late Cubist picture. Starting from this point he took a course opposite to that taken by Newman and Rothko but with similar, if more radical, results. Pollock made the *over-writing* the whole picture and in so doing rediscovered all-overness—an all-overness free of the structure of the visible world. In the best of his classical drip paintings there is a comfortable congruence between pure aesthetic regard and a surface more or less evenly articulated, between a just and even distribution of detached attention and a relative evenness of pictorial pressure.[4] The eye neither wanders aimlessly nor sticks at specific points since there is a harmony between the intensity of detail and the wholeness of the general aspect.

As Clement Greenberg has written, "Though the 'all-over' picture will, when successful, still hang dramatically on a wall, it comes very close to decoration—to the kind seen in wallpaper patterns that can be repeated indefinitely—and insofar as the 'all-over' picture remains an easel picture, which somehow it does, it infects the notion of the genre with a fatal ambiguity."[5] The easel picture has always depended not only upon unity at a single glance but on dramatic imbalance and marked variation and hierarchies of accent. Olitski has effectively reintroduced these features while exploiting the all-over picture.

Both Olitski's sprayings and Pollock's drippings are relatively impersonal applications which permit the painter to achieve large scale and to work *across* the surface (rather than inward toward the center or outward from it) without any preconceived design. Both resulted in an all-over, close-valued tonal field of more or less even tactile density yet one that is very homogeneous, airy, and transparent, and that dissolves any sense of discrete shapes. On the other hand, Pollock arrived at his dripping as a way to render his line both optical and painterly.[6] But the resulting all-overness put certain limitations on his remarkably expressive drawing, the real bearer of his

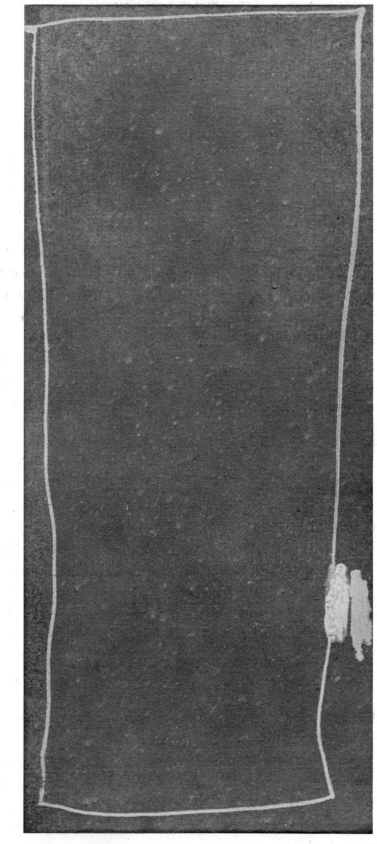

107. *Night Watch 5*. 1970.
Water-miscible acrylic on canvas, 24 × 10″.
Collection of the artist

108. *8th Loosha*. 1970.
Water-miscible acrylic on canvas, 115 1/4 × 68 1/2″. Collection of the artist

sensibility. So it was that after 1950 Pollock, like Mondrian before him, drew back. He gave up dripping and sought to give greater accentuation and variety to his painterly draughtsmanship at the expense of all-overness.[7]

Louis in his Veil paintings (pl. 52) was the first to exploit Pollock's all-over holistic field for chromatic effect. But these showed a monochrome field. Staining seemed to push painting toward pure, full-intensity hues and a Fauve-like picture. This in turn meant drawing, edges, and design. The solution of Louis and Noland after 1958 (like Mondrian before them) was to retain Pollock's holistic effect while surrendering his all-overness. Their holistic and symmetrical configurations were "non-compositional" ways to bring multiple, contrasting colors forcefully together for the viewer.

Having consigned expressive contour drawing mostly to his sculpture, Olitski in his spray paintings moved to reunite the painterly and holistic all-over picture with color. Spraying, by its very nature, results in a pictorial substance which is much more of a piece than Pollock's skeins and splatters. The latter are comparatively discrete elements, and for this reason Pollock needed to keep his articulation extremely regular.

The art historian Heinrich Wölfflin noted that the linear moves toward "multiple unity" while the painterly inclines toward what he called "unified unity." The latter is flux, "the painterly is the deliverance of the forms from their isolation," while the linear separates, isolates, articulates.[8] Creating all-overness by means of the linear enforces extreme self-limitation, as can be seen in the careers of Mondrian and Pollock. The painterly yields all-overness more easily and naturally; and this is especially true of Olitski's painterliness. Appearing as one seamless paint covering, his sprayed close-valued color fields are inherently simple, homogeneous, and

109. *1st Ally*. 1970. Water-miscible acrylic on canvas, 93 × 108 1/2". Collection Mr. and Mrs. David Mirvish, Toronto, Ont.

110. Installation of the Olitski exhibition, Winter 1971, at the David Mirvish Gallery, Toronto, Ont.

cohesive. In turn, this "unified unity" allows considerable articulation within itself. And, unlike the brushed or dripped painterliness of Abstract Expressionism, which could not easily be equally distributed, spraying gets variation of density but creates a smoothly continuous surface—one that easily admits color.[9] The reliance on different paint densities means that color shifts become—or can be made to become—identical with light and dark shifts. Moreover, by placing the main expressive emphasis on surface and color, Olitski makes available to himself far greater potential range and variety within the limits of all-overness than Pollock had available to him.

I have tried to stress that in the end Olitski came to conceive the all-over field idea separately from any specific technique (drip, pour, stain, spray). More than anyone he has grasped the idea of surface or field as an "image" of the real surface, as it were, a purely visual or virtual entity. Its identity is insured by its being a discrete, continuous unit reconstituted all at once by the palpable materiality of paint itself. But the identification of the visual and pictorial fields is never complete. This is due to the limits of the pictorial field, the actual edges of the picture. As the pictorial field becomes relatively flat and uniform it starts to call attention to these distinct limits—a feature which the visual field does not inherently possess. The viewer becomes far more aware of the discreteness of the picture as an object hanging on the wall. As a consequence, the margins of the picture seem more specific, flat, and literal as they approach the edge.[10]

As we have seen, Pollock had often given a sense of delimitedness to his fields and prevented this potential objecthood from invading his pictures at the sides by seeing to it that incident slackened in the vicinity of the actual edge of the painting; that is, he rendered these areas slightly more neutral,

111. *Radical Love—20*. 1972.
Water-miscible acrylic on canvas, 100 × 79″. Collection Mrs. Myra Davidson, Toronto, Ont.

less "painted." (In his 1958 Veils, Morris Louis did the same, but more emphatically, positively.)

Many of Olitski's earliest spray pictures of 1965 lack interior contours or lines; as the whole surface becomes a single field, the literal edges of the rectangle are felt as determinate drawing, a drawing which is somehow sculptural and pictorial at the same time.[11] Again, this possibility was available to Olitski because his sprayed all-overness was much more homogeneous than Pollock's drips. Nonetheless, to insure that the proportions and edges of the picture were experienced as drawing rather than simply neutral limits, Olitski had to restrict himself to tall, narrow formats, since only these appeared to "stamp themselves out" as pictorial.[12] Also because it is "stamped out" and pictorial—that is, emphasized—the literal shape of the rectangle now becomes a *regular* and therefore somewhat static shape. This is at odds with the mobile, shifting life of the interior incident. So the shape of the picture becomes a choice sensibly distinct from the emergent logic of the field. Or, to put it another way, the pictorial and visual fields meet abruptly.

Next Olitski made the edge more responsive to the *internal* dynamics of the picture. Even more important at this point than his discovery that the literal edge of his picture could be seen as a drawing was his prior perception that the areas near the edge provided a limited tolerance for incisive, "old-fashioned" drawing. Still, in 1965, he introduced lines of oil pastel, colored chalk, or lines caused by maskings between spray applications; in 1966, strokes of impastoed paint; and in 1972, lines made with a Magic Marker.

By diverting attention from the literal shape or edge and giving the painted surface its own edge, Olitski made the latter an image of the former. He could immediately use a wider

112. *Other Flesh-8*. 1972. Water-miscible acrylic on canvas,
86 × 51″. Collection Robert A. Rowan, Pasadena, Calif.

range of format shapes and sizes.[13] Lateral openness, compression, and release was now a variable subject to choice and control by the artist. All-overness thus became very flexible. The actual size or proportions were decided upon last, the result of the internal development of the picture. So Olitski could write, "Outer edge cannot be thought of as being in some ways within—it is the outermost extensions of the color structure. The decisions as to *where* the outer edge is, is final not initial."[14]

Bearing no shape similarity to the field, the markings can therefore relate to it more completely in terms of color and value while their immediate relation to the actual edge in terms of proximity and shape, or at least axis, means that their delimiting function is equally clear. But their specific point of occurrence along the perimeter is not determined by either of these functions. Therefore, they are freed to act compositionally, as accents.

Olitski's very flat, continuous, and homogeneous surfaces of very close value create sufficient organic unity; a balanced-out type of composition inside the picture is superfluous. The very smoothness of this unity, however, threatens that life and drama which a value-accented composition has always given to the easel picture. Often eccentrically spaced and occurring at one, two, or three sides and occasionally at the corners (but only rarely all the way around or exactly parallel with the literal edge), Olitski's marginings throw the whole surface into imbalance. They give the surface as image its own shape or make it image by giving it its own shape. These edgings render the field as a whole indeterminate, less easily graspable, and they create what is called "occult balance"—small, intense, differently articulated areas offsetting large, relatively empty ones. Sometimes erratic and abrupt, these edgings emphasize

113. *Hesperides*. 1973.
Water-miscible acrylic on canvas, 62 × 21″.
Collection Felizitas Liemersdorf, Ratingen, West Germany

114. *Absalomb Passage—10*. 1973.
Water-miscible acrylic on canvas, 102 × 65″. Collection of the artist

No depth of foreground and background, therefore contrast

and are quieted by the smooth continuity and relative homogeneity of the field to which in turn they are obviously subordinated; edge and field are not statically and uniformly juxtaposed but seem more actively and expressively responsive to each other. If Olitski's marks and value changes occurred at the center they would disrupt the continuity and the unity of the surface by reintroducing an illusion of depth, of foreground and background readings (as in Miró's work). Appearing near the edge they merely lie on or near the surface; space doesn't have room to spread out around—and by implication behind—these marks, so they merely emphasize by contrast the continuous, all-over unity of the field. At the same time they render the pictures as a whole, ambiguous and dynamic. This is even more true of the *marouflé* and irregularly shaped canvases that Olitski began in late 1979. The set, given aspect of the rectangle is completely overcome. No aspect of the picture is set or given. Everything is subject to the spontaneous choice of the artist, and the picture's status as a piece of canvas that has been covered with paint is emphasized even more than before. Almost a new species of pictorial objects, these irregularly shaped pictures have a forthrightness in declaring their physical existence that is unrivaled in painting today (pl. 134).

Since 1965, Olitski has continued to insist on a close identification between pictorial looking—the even distribution of detached attention—and the pictorial surface, on wholeness and all-overness, on image of surface and actual surface, while at the same time exploring and testing that area, at the edges, where they do not and can never coincide.[15] Also, he has exploited his discovery that a sharply restricted value range and certain kinds of painterliness result in a compelling continuum and singleness of total aspect—a singleness which in turn readmits and then suggests color and value variation. And

Olitski has been able to delimit his fields while introducing a whole new range of accentuation and drawing plus the effect of compositional liveness and dramatic imbalance into the all-over picture, a kind of picture which by its very nature would seem to exclude these very features. His style is the interface between Pollock's non-hierarchical all-overness and the dramatically articulated structures of traditional easel painting.

Modernist painting since Impressionism has been art about art, and as such its history can in part be seen as a gradual rearrangement of the conventions of representation so as to make them serve purely aesthetic ends. This point had already been perceived by Mondrian, who felt that by eliminating all but horizontal and vertical lines he had isolated the basic coordinates of all aesthetic seeing. And in a way, perhaps he had. But modernism is both more and less than Mondrian thought. It is more historical and less universal. It depends on a continual and inspired revision of what a picture is or can be. Hence, Pollock and Olitski have gone on to isolate basic facts of *pictorial seeing*. Openness, all-overness, flatness, large scale, shape of the support and an emphasis on optical color are all responses to a historical situation in which picture-viewing has become the sole touchstone and impetus for picture-making.

Not the first to arrive at the all-over picture, Olitski is also not the only painter to use it as a vehicle for color. And other painters have, here and there, quite independently, hit upon the idea of introducing pronounced changes near the margins of a more or less uniform field. But no painter has grasped more clearly or worked out more patiently the full implications of these conventions, or insisted upon them with greater consistency. In his hands they have been made to yield an extraordinary range of expressive feeling.

115. *Baphomet of Mendes*. 1973.
Water-miscible acrylic on canvas, 75 × 45″. Collection of the artist

116. *Habakkuk Radience—16*. 1973. Water-miscible acrylic on canvas, 77 × 66"
Collection Mr. and Mrs. David Mirvish, Toronto, Ont.

117. *Sisera*. 1973. Water-miscible acrylic on canvas, 23 × 17".
Collection Mr. and Mrs. David Mirvish, Toronto, Ont.

118. *Eminent Domain*. 1974.
Acrylic on canvas, 118 × 42 1/2".
Collection of the artist

119. *Yakir Five*. 1974. Water-miscible acrylic on canvas, 81 × 144″. Collection of the artist

120. *Taurus Rift—6*. 1975.
Water-miscible acrylic on canvas, 74 × 52".
Kasmin, Ltd., and Waddington and Tooth Galleries, London, England

121. *Hyksos Factor III*. 1975.
Water-miscible acrylic on canvas, 90 × 35''.
Collection Michael Steiner, New York

122. *Pleasure Ground #1*. 1975.
Water-miscible acrylic on canvas, 80 × 84″. Collection Mr. and Mrs. Philip Comstock Wherry, Chicago, Ill.

123. *Asian Massif—7.* 1975.
Water-miscible acrylic on canvas, 110 × 58″. Collection of the artist

124. *New Times—5*. 1975–76. Water-miscible acrylic
on canvas, 103 × 66″. Collection Lois and Georges de Menil, Paris, France

125. *Zin 2*. 1976.
Water-miscible acrylic on canvas, 66 × 48″. Private collection, Washington, D.C.

126. *Bashan I*. 1976. Water-miscible acrylic on canvas,
84 × 60 1/4". Collection Dr. and Mrs. Michael Stoffel, Cologne, West Germany

127. *The Greek Princess—I.* 1976.
Water-miscible acrylic on canvas, 84 × 55 1/4". Collection Dr. and Mrs. K. L. Mehra

128. *Greek Princess—8*. 1976. Water-miscible acrylic on canvas, 102 × 132." Hirshhorn Museum and Sculpture Garden, Smithsonian Institution, Washington, D.C.

130. *Kristina Type—6*. 1976.
Water-miscible acrylic on canvas,
109 × 53 1/2''.
Private collection, Boston, Mass.

131. *Nathalie Type—3*. 1976. Water-miscible acrylic on canvas, 110 × 146″. Private collection. Courtesy André Emmerich Gallery, New York

132. *Cythera—4*. 1977.
Water-miscible acrylic on canvas, 79 × 51″. Collection of the artist

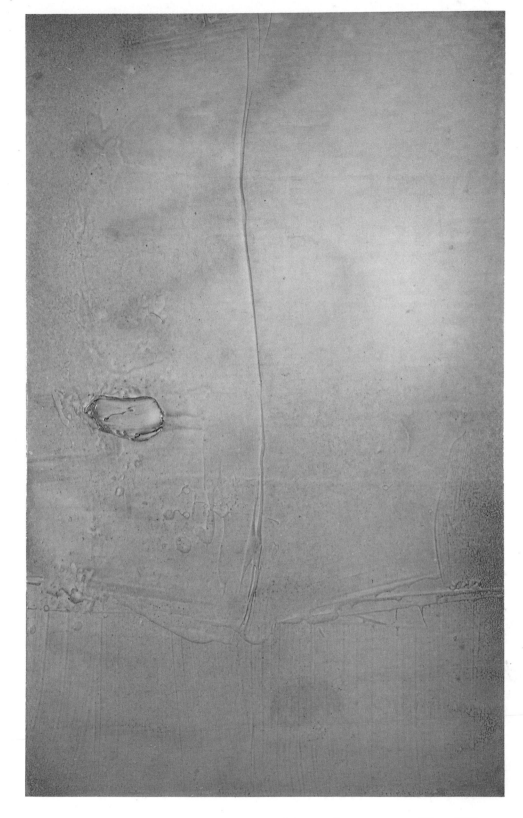

133. *Nebo-Creation—3*. 1979. Water-miscible acrylic on canvas, 60 × 36″.
Private collection. Courtesy André Emmerich Gallery, New York

134. *Magdalen Series*. 1979.
Water-miscible acrylic on canvas, 66 × 26".
Collection Clement Greenberg, New York

135. *Juno Emanation—5*. 1979. Water-miscible acrylic on canvas, 11 1/4 × 48". M. Knoedler & Co., New York

136. *First Broom of Joseph*. 1980. Water-miscible acrylic on canvas, 26 × 92". Collection Dr. and Mrs. Arthur Kay Solomon. Cambridge, Mass.

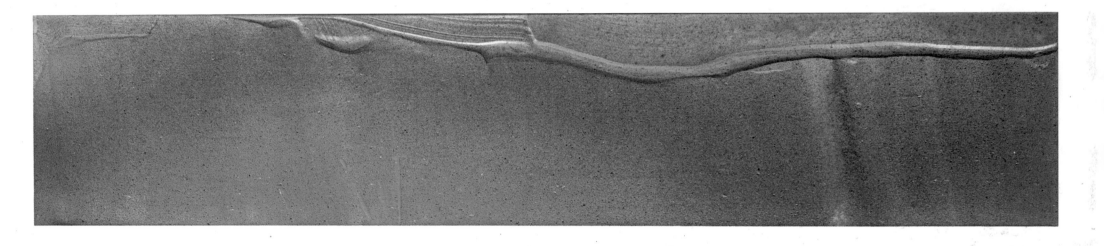

137. *Targum*. 1980. Water-miscible acrylic on canvas, 12 1/2 × 60″. Collection Lynn Martin Chusid, Marina del Rey, Calif.

LIFE DRAWINGS

138. *Laurie at Four*. 1961.
Graphite and colored crayons on white paper,
11 1/2 × 8 7/8''.
Collection of the artist

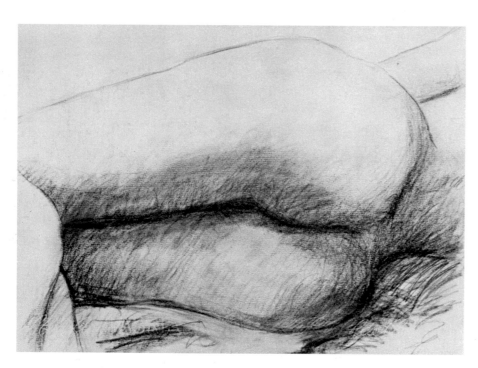

139. *Nude, Back View*. 1965. Pencil on textured paper, 9 5/8 × 13 1/8''.
Collection of the artist

140. *Seated Nude Looking Left*. c. 1968. Pencil and
graphite on white paper, 14 × 11''. Collection of the artist

141. *Nude Sleeping*. 1969.
Graphite and blue crayon on white paper,
14 × 16 7/8''.
Collection of the artist

143. *Kristina's Head*. 1976.
Charcoal on paper, 14 × 10''.
Collection Kristina Olitski

142. *Reclining Nude, Head to Knees*. Nov. 29, 1975. Charcoal on paper,
18 × 22 3/4''. Collection Richard Brown Baker, New York

NOTES TO CHAPTER TWO

1. Courbet was really the first to work all over the surface at once, or at least that is the feeling that some of his pictures convey. He often treats the whole surface with similar emphasis, thereby stressing the likeness or continuity of the paint covering *in opposition* to both the concrete particularity of three-dimensionally modeled form and to centers of narrative interest. More than anything else, this is what marks Courbet's pictures as modernist. It is clearest in those pictures in which he used white impasto in a woodland scene; white lays on top of dark. Manet, with his flat, frontal interior lighting, made light and dark, white and black seem to exist beside each other. The Impressionists, by changing to far views of bright, open spaces from close views of interiors and dark woodland interiors, justified all-over vision and eliminated the tension (by eliminating chiaroscuro). But the tension merely reappeared in the Impressionist picture now redefined as the opposition of surface *as a whole* and the world *as a whole.*

2. It is perhaps for this reason that Monet had more consistent (if less triumphant) successes with motifs such as wisteria and irises, flowers against the sky, where everything could be handled as parallel to the picture plane.

3. In conversation.

4. William Rubin has stressed the evenness of Pollock's all-over drip pictures and related them in this regard to Impressionism. See his "Jackson Pollock and the Modern Tradition," *Artforum,* Feb. 1967, pp. 14–22; Mar. 1967, pp. 28–37; Apr. 1967, pp. 18–31; May 1967, pp. 28–33. Of course, the all-over pictures of Pollock and Olitski have centers of interest and areas of subordination, but these are subtly stated within the presiding all-overness.

5. Clement Greenberg, "The Crisis of the Easel Picture," in *Art and Culture,* Boston, Beacon Press, 1961, p. 155.

6. Michael Fried, *Morris Louis, 1912–1962,* Boston, Museum of Fine Arts, 1967; and William Rubin, "Jackson Pollock and the Modern Tradition," op. cit.

7. A picture such as *Echo,* 1951 (The Museum of Modern Art, New York) lives on the tension between Pollock's will to calligraphic variation and the demands of all-overness. Also, in this picture Pollock foregoes close values in favor of sharp opposition of black and white.

8. Heinrich Wölfflin, *Principles of Art History,* New York, Dover Publications, 1956, p. 159.

9. Pollock's paint surface, the linear tangle, with its open wholeness and integration, *permitted* him to disregard the edges of his pictures; and his working over or in the picture *forced* him to disregard them. He only had to avoid a certain overlapping or cutoff feeling at the edge by pulling back slightly at that point. This tight unity of the painted area which dominates the surface and virtually or conceptually is detachable from the support is the basis of Olitski's "second" surface or field as found already in a picture like *Flaubert Red* or *Tin Lizzy Green,* but becomes even more Pollock-like later. In these two pictures the unity and identity of the field are strictly chromatic while with Pollock they are mainly linear. In both cases the unity was limiting in terms of *range.* In his post-1965 work and especially his post-1972 work, the homogeneous continuity is achieved by the material or physical continuity of paint, and less by technique per se; color and drawing (now reformulated or redefined as ridges of paint) are thus in turn freed to interact with each other.

10. This may be the reason why all pictures, including all flat abstract pictures, look better framed than unframed—at least so far.

11. Clement Greenberg, "Jules Olitski," in *XXXIII International Biennial Exhibition of Art,* Venice, 1966, p. 38. It should be noted that Olitski's early spray paintings already show drawing at the edges in the form of narrow columns of darker spray marshaled at two sides. The pictures without any edge drawing occur immediately *after* this and into 1966. Moreover, Olitski had already introduced pastel lines along the edges of some of his 1964 stain paintings and had experimented with the idea of an internal frame as early as 1951 in the drawing-board pictures.

In this regard it is also important to point to a series of black and gray pictures done by Friedel Dzubas in 1959. They are a kind of combination of Pollock's 1951 stain pictures and his all-over drip style. Dzubas stresses the margin with a scribble-like drawing that is unlike the incident within the field. That is, he conceives of the edges of the all-over field as positive. These pictures were misunderstood when shown in the fall of 1962 at the Robert Elkon Gallery in New York and Dzubas suppressed them. Olitski never saw them. Nonetheless, they show how another avant-garde painter (and a much underrated one) had grasped Olitski-like implications from Pollock's all-over fields already in the late 1950s. See my article, "Friedel Dzubas, *Dawn*," *Boston Museum Bulletin*, vol. LXXII, no. 369, 1975, pp. 27–28 (pl. 51).

12. Clement Greenberg, "Jules Olitski," p. 38.

13. The relationship between these edgings and Olitski's greater success with different formats after 1966 was first noted by Michael Fried, "Olitski and Shape," *Artforum*, Jan. 1967, pp. 20–21. Olitski has usually avoided squarish formats (and when he has employed them he has tended to have less success; see Greenberg, "Jules Olitski," p. 38). Given the character of his incident, the square is too much a fixed, self-sufficient, and neutral shape; it appears a priori and not responsive enough to the interior forces of the picture.

14. Jules Olitski, "Painting in Color," in *XXXIII International Biennial Exhibition of Art*, p. 39.

15. In certain pictures Pollock was drawn to a long narrow format. Working *across* the surface he let the shape of the picture emerge from his procedure. But his method made it difficult, if not impossible, to crop. That he projected one of his all-over surfaces onto glass, though, makes it clear that he saw his surface *primarily* as *one* thing that is at least potentially separable from the support. It is just this step, this awareness, that we do not find in European matter painting, even in Dubuffet, who also did all-over pictures.

144. Olitski in his New York studio. Spring 1980

THREE THE DEVELOPMENT OF OLITSKI'S SCULPTURE

Olitski's first important sculptures were the large, sprayed aluminum pieces he did in Saint Neots, England, in 1968, which were shown at the Metropolitan Museum of Art in the spring of the following year (pls. 145–49, 151–55). Along with the size of these sculptures (some of them were almost thirty feet long), viewers were struck at the time by their color. It was as if Olitski wanted to materialize in real space the sprayed color he used on his canvases, something which, he himself has said, was one of his ambitions. I wrote then that Olitski was trying to create in three dimensions a kind of "surfaceness" for the sake of color—not colored sculpture, but color sculpture; not a colored object, but multiple color surfaces in space.[1] While it was certainly one of Olitski's initial intentions to present large, continuous surfaces that would be effective when sprayed, it was not the only one, at least once he got started. Just as important, although I did not stress this sufficiently, was development of these sculptures in space. The latter aspect actually turned out to be both more essential than and in basic conflict with the former. Everywhere a real instinct for sculpture was asserting itself and rendering the sprayed color, if not totally irrelevant, then at least secondary or dispensable. The color seems to work somewhat better on larger, flat, simple areas, and seems most "applied" on smaller, complicated, or bulging surfaces. At best, though, it only serves to give a disembodied effect to the sculpture as a whole, and never does it exist for itself, as this *specific* hue or intensity. Probably most, if not all, of these 1968 sculptures would benefit by being monochrome. The colors tend to obscure their very real sculptural originality, their boldness, and their ambition. Nothing led up to them. There was no period of groping or learning. Olitski had hardly worked at all as a sculptor since his student days in the late

1940s and had never made abstract sculpture.[2] Yet in just seven weeks he produced twenty huge sculptures, which are surely among the most challenging done anywhere at that time.

Their general character is circular and elliptical, concave and convex, both in the parts and in their general dispositions. Together with the loose interlocking of the later ones in the series, these features remind one of Olitski's stain paintings of 1963 (the core pictures) which combine stained color and vibrant edge. They stress cutting or "weighted" contour to a degree which among stained paintings is matched only in Louis's Unfurleds (where the effect is cumulative rather than, as here, specific). And by forcing color and drawing so explicitly together they set the stage for Olitski's next pictures, the all-over stain paintings of 1964, which pretty much abolish contour drawing altogether.[3]

Olitski did not come to sculpture until well after the early sprayed pictures of 1965, those in which the shapes of the edges of the painting are experienced as *pictorial* rather than, as in previous paintings, offering simply neutral limits.[4] This new literal-pictorial, drawn character of the edges of his pictures, together with the fact that this kind of drawing was simultaneously very limiting or confining as drawing (really being only a matter of size and proportion and not at all of shape or composition) may have made Olitski more open to making sculpture. The Saint Neots pieces look as if Olitski were inspired by the pictorial, drawn quality of the literal edges of his spray pictures to create shaped surfaces in actual space; and also as if he were trying to get a new purchase on the tremulously expressive curved contours and interlocking configurations which he had surrendered in 1964. Sharp contours

145. *Bunga 45*. 1967. Aluminum with
acrylic paint, 120 × 44″. Collection Robert A. Rowan, Pasadena, Calif.

146. *Untitled*. 1968. Aluminum with
acrylic paint, 72 × 60 × 36″. Collection of the artist

147. *Untitled*. 1968.
Aluminum with acrylic paint, 72 × 36 × 72″. Collection of the artist

148. *No. 4*. 1968.
Aluminum with acrylic air-drying lacquer, 72 × 72 × 96." Collection of the artist

149. *No. 10*. 1968.
Aluminum with acrylic air-drying lacquer. Collection of the artist

are especially evident in his cutting of the dome elements. The shaped domes are combined with crenulated sheets which were also shaped in various ways.[5]

Looking back, I think that Olitski wanted everything at once: a pictorial shaping of edges, rounded configurations, broad continuous surfaces of sprayed color, and an additive, highly differentiated—and consequently discontinuous—vocabulary of elements. Add to all of this that Olitski was seeking to embody in these sculptures a very specific spatial experience. "When I was just about to make those earlier sculptures, later shown at the Metropolitan Museum, I was visiting Avignon. The Palace of the Popes was closed that day and I could not get inside. So I had this marvelous experience in walking around the gardens and the steps of the palace. You did not know where the level ground was, you never knew—at one point low, at another point high. You never knew quite where you were, everything being relative to everything else, so that there is no norm, so to speak, no floor. I wanted to try to get something related to that feeling—of the sculpture related to ground and coming out of the ground—and never quite knowing where one is in relation to either one."[6]

Strictly speaking, this is more a landscape or architectural experience than a sculptural one; it is an experience more of space than of form. And this feeling or something like it does occur in the Saint Neots sculptures despite the fact that they manifestly rest on the same flat, horizontal surface as the viewer, i.e., the floor of the room. Again, it is mainly the cut-domes which create this impression of the sculpture emerging from or sinking into the ground rather than merely sitting upon it. More than one observer has noticed that viewing these sculptures is very like viewing a landscape.

150. Anthony Caro. *Early One Morning*. 1962.
Acrylic on steel, 114 × 244 × 132″.
The Tate Gallery, London, England

Part of this landscape feeling, too, has to do with the syntax, the stringing out of the elements in a low, side-by-side horizontal extension. This syntax as well as the vocabulary—insofar as it is constituted of sharply differentiated, discrete parts—relate Olitski to the English sculptor Anthony Caro (pl. 150). It is a vocabulary and syntax that in the end, I think, thwarted Olitski's two main ambitions: to create a sculptural equivalent for the broad continuous chromaticism of his paintings, and, simultaneously, to find a sculptural equivalent for his experience at Avignon. Neither of these ambitions is sculptural per se, and each is in potential conflict with the other. The effort to create a complicated spatial experience is, finally, at odds with the desire to reduce sculpture to pure surface. In his next series of sculptures, Olitski not only devised a new vocabulary and a new syntax, but also eliminated applied color—all for the sake of finding a truly sculptural equivalent of his spatial idea.

Despite his use of a Caroesque vocabulary and syntax in the Saint Neots series, Olitski did not, in the actual joining of the parts, adopt Caro's subtle tiltings, tippings, anglings, and touchings of elements, but made each piece sit directly on the ground, manifestly supporting nothing but itself. He kept the relationships between parts purely visual or pictorial, not at all a matter of weight or tension. These sculptures possess more of the ground area and are less open than Caro's. This impulse to "possess" the ground remains characteristic of all Olitski's sculpture. But it was only in the later pieces of the series, *Whipout* (pl. 153), *Heartbreak of Ronald and William* (pl. 154), and *Wheels Up* (pl. 151), that he began to substitute for simple juxtaposition the kind of intersecting and especially interlocking which are found in his 1963 core pictures. And in the very last piece, *Ohel of Volya* (pl. 155), which

151. Installation of exhibition at the Metropolitan Museum of Art, New York. Spring 1969. Background: *Whipsaw*. 1968. Acrylic and air-drying lacquer on aluminum, 36 × 252 × 138″. Private collection, Boston, Mass. Foreground: *Wheels-up*. 1968. Acrylic and air-drying lacquer on aluminum, 328 × 40 1/2 × 84″. Promised gift of William S. Rubin to the Whitney Museum of American Art, New York

152. *Whipsaw*. 1968. Aluminum with acrylic air-drying lacquer, 36 × 252 × 138".
Private collection, Boston, Mass. Installation at the Metropolitan Museum of Art, New York. Spring 1969

was done later than the others and falls somewhat out of the series as a whole, Olitski made a new departure.

The very first one of the series is a tall, rectangular sheet, like his canvases, that was simply curved so that it would stand by itself, and then sprayed on both sides (pl. 146). "Edging" was added as though he were finishing one of his pictures. Olitski then developed the other pieces adding and linking curved or "rolled" surfaces, hence their general floor plan of strung out, interlocking curves. These forms, while originally resulting from the simplest possible means of support, also relate to Olitski's feeling for shape and form (as is clear from his 1963 pictures). So he developed them laterally in plan, and then, as the series continued, also in profile. These, too, are curvilinear and interlocking. In general, they are lower and have more of a landscape feeling. This is what makes *Ohel of Volya*, the last one of the series, so unusual, really the beginning of something new.

Like the drawings for sculptures which Olitski did in late 1968 and early 1969, *Ohel of Volya* shows an interest in involuted, climbing, spiral forms. At that time, Olitski mentioned to me that he wanted somehow to express the feeling of a spiral staircase in sculptural terms.[7] *Ohel of Volya* combines spatial ideas derived from the architectural and landscape-like experience at Avignon with the architectural idea of a spiral staircase. It is vertical (eight feet high) and concentric, rather than horizontal and lateral. Resembling a work of architecture more than a landscape, this piece (certainly the most inventive and even outrageous of the series) is based on a unique concept. The whole is like some round shelter, with an exterior ramp and flat disks proliferating in and around it. Everything seems to be in a state of coming together or slipping apart. The vocabulary has been simplified—flat or curved sheets of

153. *Whip-out*. 1968.
Aluminum with acrylic air-drying lacquer, 60 × 252 × 144".
Hirshhorn Museum and Sculpture Garden, Smithsonian Institution, Washington, D.C.

154. *Heartbreak of Ronald and William*. 1968. Aluminum with acrylic air-drying lacquer, 48 × 312 × 186". Collection of the artist

155. *Ohel of Volya*. 1968. Aluminum with acrylic air-drying lacquer, 105 × 180 × 144″. Collection Mr. and Mrs. David Mirvish, Toronto, Ont.

156. *Untitled*. Summer 1970.
Mild steel, rusted and lacquered, 10 × 54 × 54".
Collection of the artist

cut steel—and the work is without closed or concealed volume. Both its plan and elevation conspire to define and appropriate an autonomous spatial volume within which the piece establishes its own frame of reference and system of shifting spatial levels. All the levels and edges appear to escape alignment with the horizontality of the floor (or the verticality of the wall) and the floor itself is hardly visible on the "inside" of the sculpture. Olitski here lets his spatial idea—shifting and climbing levels, none of which is privileged—determine the vocabulary and syntax of the piece, which seems suspended between a desire to spread outward and extend into space and a desire to close in upon itself, to enclose space: between the centrifugal and centripetal. Olitski was concerned with the continuity and relationships of surfaces rather than the relationships of discrete parts. For this purpose, concentricity and building upward turned out to be more useful than horizontal, additive extension.

Soon after the completion of *Ohel of Volya* in 1969 Olitski started his concentric "ring" sculptures, which he worked on in the summers from 1970 through 1973. At first encounter, these look like direct three-dimensional translations of the core pictures, not just in shape vocabulary, but in total configuration. Yet the ring series should probably also be seen as a new synthesis of the Avignon and spiral staircase ideas. A variety of shifting and concentric levels now occurs *inside* the sculpture while the sculpture *as a whole* seems to emerge from or sink into the ground. Usually irregular, the low perimeter ring measures itself against the plane of the ground around it, while on the inside, the ground, when visible at all, is absorbed into the shallow but autonomous interior system of spatial play. This sense of shifting levels and thus of the ground plane beneath the sculpture becoming ambiguous and illusive, or even dissolving altogether, is heightened if one moves around the piece. If in the Saint Neots sculptures Olitski tried to convey a preexisting spatial feeling by reproducing it (they *are* landscape-like), here he finds a true abstract sculptural *equivalent* for this same feeling.

It is instructive to see these sculptures, as well as the earlier ones, in relation to Olitski's painting. Writing of the painted aluminum sculptures, Olitski has said, "Sculptural shape is to the ground support what pictorial shape is to painting support."[8] The ring pieces are even more painting-like in this regard, since they seem to be a direct transposition of the core pictures into three dimensions, treating the ground plane, or ground plan, almost like the picture plane. Their sense of autonomy defined by explicit perimeters, their relative lack of elevation, and the way they establish their own internal, closed-off system of relations further link them to painting. Again, like a picture, they are completely visible all at once (though to get the full effect of shifting and turning levels one must walk around them). It is as if to express semi-architectural and semi-landscape spatial experience, and to combine these in sculptural terms—that is as a virtual object—Olitski has had to make sculpture more pictorial or picture-like. The ring sculptures are also more sculptural than the Saint Neots sculptures. They abandon color and so relinquish an insistence on surface as such. Seeking to define an internal, self-referential spatial system, Olitski has now made his sculptures primarily a question of drawing; emphasis is on overall shape and then on edge and plane.

As we have already had occasion to note, color and texture tend to be seen more easily at the light end of the value scale where they can therefore more easily receive the main emphasis. At the darker end of the scale, these features take

157. *Lot's Draw.* 1970.
Mild steel, rusted and oiled, h. 16", diam. 137 1/2".
Collection of the artist

158. *Untitled.* Spring/Summer 1970. Mild steel, rusted and lacquered, 40 × 87 × 88''. Collection of the artist

second place to the sharpening of light and dark differences (this presumably because it is harder for us to see here, so we revert to the simplest and clearest way of seeing, i.e., in light and dark). This has meant that most paintings emphasizing color since Impressionism have been high key. It is certainly true of Olitski's, and it also accounts for why he has generally had far more success at that end of the scale. But sculpture is different. Here, an emphasis on light value and applied color— and certainly color as uneven paint densities, like his sprayings —puts the emphasis on surface texture. But Olitski was increasingly coming to see sculpture as drawing. Only with a darker, more uniform surface could the emphasis be shifted away from surface and toward edge drawing, silhouette, light and dark. It is no accident, then, that he switched to unsprayed rolled steel at this point.

If Olitski's first spray paintings make the issue of contour drawing totally explicit, it is the centered core pictures in which he is most clearly the draughtsman. So it was natural that he should return to the concentric core idea when, in the ring series, his sculpture came to be about drawing rather than color.

Concentric circles (or the spiral) became, like the cube, one of the archetypal geometric forms associated with Minimal art.[9] But instead of merely presenting it representationally—i.e., for its "primariness" per se—Olitski used it as it was first used in his and others' paintings, as a starting point, something against which or from which the piece develops. Concentricity does not constitute a mere statement or assertion, but is a theme that permits and encourages sensibility and invention. Variation, moreover, is not, as with the Minimalists, only a question of size and material. Olitski returned to wholeness as a way to express a spatial idea. He was interested in differences

159. *Jonah's Promise* (first version). 1971–72.
Mild steel, h. 30", diam. 58".
Collection of the artist

160. *Hybrid T*. 1972. Cor-ten steel, h. 2′6″, diam. 28′. Collection of the artist

161. *Benghi*. 1972. Mild steel, rusted and oiled, h. 120", diam. 98". Collection of the artist

162–163. *Honey*. 1972. Mild steel, h. 16″, diam. 97″. Collection of the artist

of elevation, spacing, and proportion, and he put great emphasis on slight irregularities and nonalignments. All of this is experienced as a departure from and interplay with concentricity; the idea is not exhausted at first glance.

The first ring sculpture, *Lot's Draw* (pl. 157), does have something very minimal about it, and it is the only one which looks at all schematic and symmetrical. As such, it is uniquely instructive in succeeding where so much Minimal art fails. It shows how much better most Minimal art could have been if the artists had some real sense of proportion and shape, and, above all, if they had made some effort to deal with the relation of the sculpture to the ground. In *Lot's Draw*, Olitski used sloping surfaces to create the impression that the sculpture is scooping into (or sliding out of) the ground. In any event, Olitski immediately began to explore the concentric idea by making rings into irregular ovals or tilting them in contrasting directions.[10] As in the core pictures, the resulting feeling is of interlocking (as sculptures they interlock in their shallow elevation as well as in their spread-out ground plan) and of the different rings rotating in opposite directions. There are some ten of these low ring pieces, all concentric rather than true spirals, although several have a spiraling effect. They measure between 58 and 171 inches in diameter, except for *Hybrid T* (pl. 160), which is 30 by 28 inches. Since the guiding idea does not emerge from the vocabulary but is given by a single a priori gestalt, the ring series forms much more of a coherent group than the sprayed series. Some show an internal density and jamming (*Honey*, pls. 162, 163; *Hybrid T*) which is new to constructed sculpture, while others are extraordinarily spare—and elegant—consisting of only two large, low rings (*Redemption Secret, Alcestis*, pls. 168, 169). The rings can seem to hang loosely above the floor (*Chinese Cassandra*, pl.

166) or, in one of the most successful works, to be cut into a ramp form as if by some huge cookie cutter (*Untitled*, pl. 167).

By enclosing a space all their own, the ring sculptures "distance" the viewer in that they convey a strong sense of occupied territory. But their ground-hugging, shallow character explicitly rejects any hint of rhetoric. And since the holistic configuration exists for the sake of multiple, dense, internal relationships, it is the opposite of so much Minimal art, which claims to use holism to *reduce* internal relationships and by implication make the work relate first to its environment. It ought to be noted, too, that these works are quite different from those of Anthony Caro, whose influence has been so pervasive in contemporary abstract sculpture. A typical Caro is expansively additive, develops laterally, is centerless, and deliberately avoids an enclosing profile. What at first seems multiple emerges as a new kind of object. With an Olitski, one is confronted with an obvious, simple a priori unit or unity. The vocabulary is simpler and more uniform. The ring sculptures are like Olitski's earlier sculptures in that they work not in terms of balance, weight, and vectors, as in Caro's case, but only visually and pictorially, as it were, by means of drawing and composition. In some ways they are much closer to the mode of unity and the kind of experience associated with recent color painting than with recent constructed sculpture.

A conception of sculpture derived ultimately from two dimensions is bound to remain limiting in the long run. Wholeness is a spin-off of all-overness and belongs to painting, not to sculpture. Also, so much emphasis on ground plan means that the sculpture, while "in the round," does not fully exploit the third dimension. Another problem or limitation of the ring idea has to do with scale. Since these sculptures are so self-referential, Olitski had to make sure that the work did

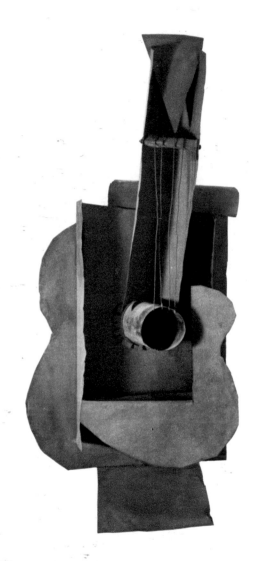

164. Pablo Picasso. *Guitar.* 1912.
Sheet metal and wire, 30 1/2 × 13 1/8 × 7 5/8".
The Museum of Modern Art, New York.
Gift of the artist

165. *Tombola*. 1972. Mild steel, rusted and oiled, h. 13 1/2'', diam. 98''. Collection of the artist

166. *Chinese Cassandra*. 1972. Cor-ten steel, h. 17'', diam. 180''. Collection of the artist

not develop its own sense of scale, like a model for something else, but retained a direct and immediate relationship to the viewer. To this end, he found ways to underline the composite, segmented character of the rings—the fact that they are made of simple pieces of steel—and as the series developed he increasingly de-emphasized closed shape or volume and made each ring of simple, single curved sheets set upright (*Alcestis, Redemption Secret, Hybrid T*). Large, thin, curving sheets of steel do not have to seem rigid, but can appear bendable and elastic. As with the slight irregularities Olitski favors and the way that parts of his sculptures often don't quite align with each other, these sheets or planes then can act to loosen and relax the geometry of the conception. Here, choice of material counts as "touch" or "sensibility." Moreover, used like this, steel declares its own literalness and materiality.

Considerations like these played a part in the very last ring sculptures, which are tall and tublike. They engage more fully with three dimensions in that they are now commanding in elevation. It is almost as if Olitski were exaggerating one characteristic of the low ring pieces: their tendency to, as he puts it, "turn their back" on the viewer. His painting has indeed often had this characteristic—an initial blank, deadpan look. Quality results exactly because this seeming blankness itself becomes positively expressive. It is a range of feeling that is especially available to flat and all-over painting, and it orig-inated in the pictures of Jackson Pollock and Barnett Newman, but has been exploited by Olitski most of all.

This is another effect that Minimalism tried to capture for sculpture. But there, as well as in much Minimalist painting of the later '60s and '70s, blankness and deadpanness don't become expressive but remain merely a "look." In fact, it has become *the* "in" look, just as agitated spontaneity was the in

167. *Untitled.* 1973.
Cor-ten steel, h. 22", diam. 171".
Collection of the artist

168. *Redemption Secret*. 1973. Mild steel, h. 17 1/2″, diam. 115″. Collection of the artist

169. *Alcestis*. 1973. Cor-ten steel, 24 × 95 × 86″. Collection of the artist

170. *Maenads*. 1973. Cor-ten steel, h. 48″, diam. 95″. Collection of the artist

171. *Ariadne*. 1973. Cor-ten steel, h. 52 1/2″, diam. 96″. Collection of the artist

look of the '50s. Everywhere we have been offered forbidding or unyielding blankness or deadness or flat-footedness. Almost always, though, this has been only a sign of seriousness and uncompromisingness available to every art student. Almost always this look fails to transcend itself and ends up a period look—our period look—not something achieved, but something succumbed to or exploited. The mere look of the anti-art is as arty as any blandishment.[11]

Olitski's tub pieces of 1973—*Ariadne* (pl. 171), *King Kong* (pls. 172–74), and *Maenads* (pl. 170)—certainly have a blank look. They are, as Olitski likes to say, just "plopped" down in a deliberately flat-footed or deadpan way, and with their "backs" to the viewer. Above all, this emphasizes their literalness, and it undercuts all velleities toward an autonomous scale. But Olitski was not satisfied with the experience of objecthood per se. He immediately reintroduced contour drawing and varied spatial levels by freely scalloping the edges of these tall, concentric walls. Almost like a parody of drawing, the edges are certainly in the general spirit of these sculptures. But in the main I find that the tall rings, despite their presence and mystery, stay too much inside the limiting aspects of the ring idea and its relatively restricted possibilities for relationships. They overstress the fact that they have a hidden inside. This is the effect of traditional, figurative sculpture and pottery where multiple, curved surfaces allow the outside to be related to—in the same sense as being expressive of—the inside. Olitski's inspiration did not take him in this direction. But the tub sculptures do show that Olitski was now interested in developing his sculpture vertically in a more fully three-dimensional way. (We have already seen that Caro's way of developing a sculpture laterally and horizontally proved unsuitable for what Olitski had to say.)

172–74. *King Kong*. 1973.
Cor-ten steel, 60 × 112 × 101". Collection of the artist

175. *Untitled*. 1973. Mild steel, rusted and laquered, 14 × 94″. Collection of the artist

176. *Untitled*. 1973. Cor-ten steel, 18 × 96 × 48". Collection of the artist

An observation made by his friend, the critic Clement Greenberg, started Olitski on his next series in 1974. Greenberg noticed a group of simple curved sheets stacked more or less neatly to one side of Olitski's sculpture pad in Shaftsbury, Vermont. They were to be used in the assembly of some tall ring pieces. Greenberg remarked that they were interesting just the way they were. Always open to suggestions or criticisms from those whom he respects—he is remarkably undefensive about such things—Olitski began thinking about Greenberg's observation. Then he had the idea of piling this group of sheets *on top* of a low ring sculpture and piling another "story" of tall ring segments on top of that. The result was *Greenberg Variations* (pls. 178–80), which became the prototype for Olitski's third and most recent series of sculptures. They show a new way of dealing with thin, single, curved or straight steel sheets piled up or set on edge; instead of using them as parts of larger units, he stacked them in tiers one above the other. This proved a strikingly simple way to achieve a more literal and more open sculpture, one that was vertical, developable, and fully spatial.

The fact that each tier of the stacked sculptures, composed of broad, curved or straight planes, is conceived as a separate story that has to support the one above makes for a built-in cursiveness. Stacking and piling is an additive structural idea, and as such less predetermining than a holistic form. So, while constituting a discrete series, these stacked pieces are more variable than the ring sculptures. And they are less object-like, less "one thing"; as a conglomerate of parts they are free to develop vertically. They also show Olitski's taste for the most matter-of-fact and at the same time loose structural relationships together with curving, interlocking, visual ones. And they

177. *Jonah's Promise* (second version). 1971–74. Mild steel, 46 × 84 1/4 × 84 1/4″. Collection of the artist

continue his tendency to think of sculpture in terms of levels and their relationships.

As we have said, in his pictures Olitski has come to the simplest possible, most matter-of-fact way of making an abstract painting; he merely covers the rectangle with paint. His sculpture shows the same kind of brilliant simplicity, or perhaps one should say inspired "dumbness." To make a sculpture in the round he simply makes it of or sets it on concentric rings.[12] To make a vertical sculpture he merely piles the pieces one on top of another. Finding and accepting the simplest, most logical solution is a feature we find in the great masters of the past. It usually makes the artist both influential and hard to follow. And this certainly has been true of Olitski. As the young painter Darryl Hughto has remarked, he is both a very wide and a very narrow door. Along with his playfulness and his relaxed and generous sensuality, Olitski's radical simplicity has been the most distinctive characteristic of his work so far. And, of course, these qualities are all related, since his holistic conceptions are simple and wide so as to allow his relaxed and loose way of working to count as sensibility and to let sensibility have the widest possible latitude. Michael Fried has remarked, "Olitski is chiefly intent on proving how much of his own sensibility can be made valid in terms of modernist paintings."[13] The same can be said of Olitski the sculptor.

Greenberg Variations has a marked front and back. The next pieces in the series, *Anchorite* (pl. 182) and *Also Admah* (pl. 183), capitalize more on the all-around spatial potential of the stacking idea in that they are based on tiers of roughly parallel curving sheets that criss-cross each other at right, or at least opposing, angles on each level. In *Ur* (pl. 186) Olitski

178–80. *Greenberg Variations*. 1974.
Cor-ten steel, 122 × 163 × 124″.
Hirshhorn Museum and Sculpture Garden,
Smithsonian Institution, Washington, D.C.

181. *Untitled*. 1974. Cor-ten steel, c. 60 × 108 × 108″. Collection of the artist

182. *Anchorite*. 1974.
Cor-ten steel, 61 × 96 × 102″. Collection of the artist

183. *Also Admah* (earlier version). 1974.
Cor-ten steel, 61 1/2 × 108 × 110″. Collection of the artist

184–85. *Shechinah Temptations*. 1976. Cor-ten steel, 72 × 130 × 66″. Collection Lois and Georges de Menil, Paris, France

used straight sheets for one level and curved for the next. Sometimes one tier is piled flatly, the next set vertically on edge. Usually the whole configuration is closed, roughly rectangular in silhouette, and rectangular or circular in ground plan.

All these works unfold and fold, open and close from level to level as one proceeds around them. Rude and simple, they are also complex, evocative. Throughout the changes of vocabulary, orientation, proportion, and number of levels, Olitski retains the "dumb" effect of a simple pile. One story may be cantilevered out, but there is no tipping or tilting or leaning of planes—no diagonals—and no sense of one part or plane as more structural or more in tension than another. Essentially, the planes are all set at right angles to each other and to the room; some shift in axis but not in elevation, so there is no feeling of anything built up but only piled on. Since the planes are piled flatly or rest on an edge or point, there is not much internal sense of load or strain, of weight or pressure, but there is the massive presence of the steel pile as a whole. The parts remain very much themselves—broad planes of Cor-ten steel—making the sculpture itself very direct and physical. On the other hand, in most of these layers broad planes rest on smaller ones and everything floats on a shallow ring (or more recently on a corrugated piece). Above, the pieces often seem hinged, capable of swinging free, and the whole, like a house of cards, feels light, precarious, or temporary (as if it *could* be made of cardboard).

Most recently Olitski tried stacking the sheets with their broad sides horizontal rather than vertical. Again he alternated tiers of curved and straight sheets, and he began including levels of corrugated ones. Corrugated sheets give dimension to the sculptures stacked this way, and reintroduce the continuous, wavy, whimsical drawing—almost childlike in its insistence—of the tubs, giving more springiness and lightness to the potential inertness and dead weight of the pile. They add to the weightless, floating feeling, as well as an accordian-like spatial thrust and movement. The ground plan here is square or rectilinear.

By comparison with the recent stacked pieces, the earlier ones, with their upright sheets, seem almost elegant. In *Lippis de Salomé* (pl. 189) and *Réjane Possessed* (pl. 188), the effect is even more that of a "mere" pile, of a casual or accidental or provisional stack of steel sheets. As such, they are fully sculptural equivalents for the feeling Olitski was aiming at in the tubs: flat-footed, deadpan, artlessly plopped down. But Olitski's drawing runs throughout these pieces and into three dimensions. It is primarily this graphic character, which all the pieces share with Olitski's other sculptures, that makes them so pictorial, so much a painter's sculpture. They are about planes and drawing: planes which overlap or interlock or slide past each other, and line as edge. In them Olitski's contour drawing varies from the tautly or loosely cursive through the austere and spare to the funky scallop or the child's stubborn scribble.[14] And these sculptures are about drawing in another sense—in the sense of light and dark, chiaroscuro. Since the tiers are at right angles to each other and to the ground, these sculptures create a range of light to deep dark heretofore unavailable to abstract constructed steel sculpture. And their sharp and then subtle shifts of light and dark strengthen and then soften the boldness of their drawing. Yet, for all this pictorialism, they very much occupy their own space.[15] Rectangular or circular in ground plan and more or less rectangular and self-contained in profile, they distance the viewer. Some, such as *Shechinah Temptations* (pls. 184, 185), are houselike, while others, such as *Ur,* are almost

186. *Ur*. 1976. Cor-ten steel, 78 × 157 × 151″. Collection of the artist

187. Installation of the Olitski sculpture show at the Museum of Fine Arts, Boston, 1977.
Left to right: *Réjane Possessed*, 1977; *Shechinah Temptations*, 1976; *Lippis de Salomé*, 1977

188. *Réjane Possessed*. 1977.
Cor-ten steel, 60 × 116 × 82″. Collection of the artist

189. *Lippis de Salomé*. 1977.
Cor-ten steel, 52 × 135 × 123″. Installed at the Hirshhorn Museum, 1977. Collection of the artist

more like a spatial event than a sculptural object per se. The architectural and the pictorial conspire to produce an original sculptural statement.

As we have noted, the stacked pieces embody a feeling which originally, at least, was a pictorial one.[16] The idea of piling sculptures one upon the other in tiers originated in Olitski's work on *Jonah's Promise* (pl. 159), a small, squat ring or tub piece (22.1/2 by 58 inches) that was shown at Knoedler Contemporary Art in 1973. Later he became dissatisfied with it. Then, while visiting the Louvre in the spring of 1974, he saw the base of an Ionic column from the large temple of Apollo at Didyma which, for some reason, had been hollowed out (pl. 190). It gave him the idea of putting *Jonah's Promise* on a large, square box (pl. 177). The proportions are such that the result does not look like the base of a column or a sculpture on a base, but like two Minimalist sculptures, one growing out of the other. The box makes the depth of the ring's cavity uncertain, ambiguous, elusive, like the other ring sculptures. Brancusi had discovered that when a sculpture is radically simplified, the base, rather than merely setting it off, becomes more like a part of the sculpture itself. In his efforts to capitalize on this discovery, Brancusi often fell into ambiguity or artiness. But certain of his works go a step further and create the effect of several sculptures piled one atop the other (*Pasarea Maiastra*, 1910; *The Sorceress*, 1916–22; *Adam and Eve*, 1921; as well as such architecture-inspired works as *Boundary Marker*, 1945). These might be seen as monolithic versions of what Olitski is doing in constructed steel sculpture, with the qualification that with Brancusi the top piece is usually the climax, whereas Olitski usually avoids this effect.

Piling tiers on top of one another—like turning a sculpture upside down, which Olitski also does sometimes—was possi-

190. Base of Ionic column from the large Temple of Apollo at Didyma. The Louvre, Paris, France

191. *Untitled*. 1977. Cor-ten steel, 108 × 72 × 48″. Collection of the artist

192. *Zarathustra*. 1977. Aluminum, 72 × 93 × 60″. Collection of the artist

193. Photo-montage in preparation for a sculpture, August 1974

ble because of Olitski's open and unorthodox way of working. He does not construct, as such; he juxtaposes and piles. The relationships are wholly visual ones. He is not inspired by structural problems, nor does he come to sculptural ideas by finding a specific piece or element or by moving elements around. In fact, he hardly gets involved with the process of making at all anymore. He only works on sculpture two or three times each year, and then only for a few days at a time. Since the Saint Neots sculptures all his pieces have been totally assembled and finished by assistants. Olitski never handles the steel himself.[17] Usually he makes a rapid drawing with colored crayons and indicates the sizes and thicknesses of the pieces he wants. Also, he has used photo montages of his own works, cutting up photos of his previous sculptures and combining them in new configurations (pl. 193). Once his assistants, working from these sketches, have assembled and fixed the sculptures in a temporary way, he goes to Bennington to see if he wants to make changes, leaves instructions, and looks at the sculpture again the next time he is there. He usually has his assistants work on two or three sculptures at the same time. Occasional, even casual, his approach makes for a distance from the medium which is in perfect accord with the way he approaches sculpture generally. Often the feeling he wants or even the basic concept exists in his mind even before he makes a sketch. Just as often inspiration comes while making a sketch. But in either case the conception comes before rather than during the actual making. This is very different from the way Olitski makes paintings or from the way sculpture is generally made today by constructivist-type sculptors. It bears certain analogies with the way Minimalist sculpture is made and, as I will try to show in the next chapter, it is an approach which is available thanks in part to recent developments in painting.

194. *Untitled*. 1977. Soft steel, 70 × 92 × 71″. Collection of the artist.

195–96. *Contropposto*. 1978–79. Cor-ten steel, 92 × 118 × 104″. Collection Gallaudet College, Washington, D.C.

NOTES TO CHAPTER THREE

1. "The Sculpture of Jules Olitski," *Artforum*, Apr. 1969, pp. 55–59. The following two chapters are a revised version of the introduction to the exhibition catalogue, *Olitski: New Sculpture*, Boston, Museum of Fine Arts, 1977.

2. The English sculptor Anthony Caro offered Olitski the use of his studio in London to do sculpture. Olitski's first response was to do drawings, but then he decided that he wanted to work in a more spontaneous way, and so ordered a large amount of materials, a great assortment of parts. In this way, he could work freely and directly, as Caro did in his sculpture and as Olitski himself did in his own paintings. But the space required to house this large supply of big parts made it impossible to use Caro's studio, so Olitski rented another studio, really a factory, in Saint Neots near Cambridge, England. It is interesting, though, that when turning to sculpture Olitski's *first* impulse was to *draw*, to conceive on paper, and this is the approach he returned to after the Saint Neots pieces.

3. See Michael Fried, "New York Letter," *Art International*, Mar. 1964, pp. 40–42.

4. See Clement Greenberg, "Jules Olitski," in *XXXIII International Biennial Exhibition of Art*, Venice, 1966, p. 38.

5. The tubes and rods were the least effective elements, and Olitski abandoned them early on in the series.

6. Friedrich Bach, "Interview mit Jules Olitski," *Kunstwerk*, May 1975, pp. 14–24 (see p. 216 of this volume).

7. He also remembers becoming fascinated by a children's slide in the form of a spiral that he saw in a playground.

8. "On Sculpture," *The Metropolitan Museum of Art Bulletin*, Apr. 1969, p. 366.

9. The use of a spiral form in abstract sculpture, of course, goes back to Tatlin's *Monument to the Third International*, 1919–20.

10. In their loose conjunction of relatively thin sheets and their use of irregularity, they can remind one a bit of Picasso's metal *Guitar*, 1912, in The Museum of Modern Art (pl. 164).

11. One of these ring pieces, *Redemption Secret*, bears a resemblance to a work by the Minimalist artist, Donald Judd. Judd's *Untitled*, 1971, was shown at the Sixth Guggenheim International in 1971. Olitski never saw this sculpture, and had been working on the concentric idea since immediately after *Ohel of Volya* (1968–69). In the winter of 1969–70 he did two small clay models on canvas board which were the prototypes of the ring pieces begun the following summer. Judd's work, certainly one of his best, made an effort to relate the sculpture to its environment, the spiraling Guggenheim interior. The edge of the inside circle conformed to the slope of the Guggenheim ramp; the edge of the outside circle was level. Olitski's approach was exactly the opposite. He wanted to express an architectural and landscape (i.e., spatial and environmental) experience in an autonomous, self-enclosed work. Judd usually aims to be flat-footed and unambiguous, but the Guggenheim interior was so powerful that it forced him to become suggestive and illusive (more like Olitski).

12. Since constructed sculpture is made of discrete parts, it has not usually been continuously round like so much older representational sculpture, which has a continuous outer skin. Gabo and Pevsner, who worked with warped surfaces, were exceptions. Olitski gets roundness in the most natural and direct way possible. Again one thinks of Picasso's *Guitar* (see note 10), with its dark metal, its emphasis on planar rectangularity, its bladelike edges, and its deeply shadowed spatial slots between edges, now rendered abstract, totally in the round (some, like *Ur*, pl. 186, have no privileged view), monumental (in *Ur*, almost architectural in scale), and powerfully present.

13. Michael Fried, *Three American Painters*,

Cambridge, Mass., Fogg Art Museum, Harvard University, 1965, p. 33.

14. This range of draughtsmanship is visible in the sketches for the sculptures as well as in his early, post-1964 stain paintings.

15. Even when working with sprayed color, though, Olitski was never pictorial in the sense, say, that David Smith was pictorial, remaining oriented to the flat, frontal "picture plane." From the first, Olitski's sculpture has been fully spatial in the sense that it is in the round and appropriates large areas for itself, i.e., it is always spatial or sculptural in ground plan.

16. From another point of view, stacking or piling is just the vertical equivalent of juxtaposing the pieces horizontally, which Olitski did in the Saint Neots pieces and in the ring pieces. It is the simplest possible way to combine elements in space. Also, it should be noted that the actual joining of these sculptures—bolts and spot welds—is also very straightforward. These pieces are not at all self-consciously crafted.

17. In the Saint Neots pieces, Olitski used anodized aluminum. It already had color, took spray paint easily, and was light and so could be moved around with a minimum of effort. In the ring pieces, he switched to mild steel, lacquered, and later in the series to Cor-ten steel. The latter can be left outdoors and does not need care. It rusts to a certain stage and stops.

197. Olitski with Clement Greenberg (left) and the author (right) at a sculpture workshop, Bennington, Vt. 1977

FOUR OLITSKI'S SCULPTURE AND MODERNISM

When a painter of Olitski's stature begins to make sculpture, and when the sculpture is as ambitious and assertive as his, one invariably wants to ask about the relationship between the two activities. Other abstract painters have begun to make sculpture in recent years: Kenneth Noland, Larry Poons, Helen Frankenthaler, to name only three. Meanwhile, Minimalism, which has more or less dominated sculpture, also had its beginnings in painting, and most of its practitioners began as painters. Of course, it is hardly the first time that painters have worked in three dimensions. Indeed, many if not most of the best modern sculptures have been done by artists who were primarily painters. There is an obvious reason for this. Since the beginning of modernism, since Courbet and Manet, painting has oriented itself toward flatness at the expense of depicted sculptural form. Painters who have a strong inclination to draw sculpturally have found a natural outlet in sculpture itself. Certainly this was the case with Renoir and Degas, the two sculptor-draughtsmen among the Impressionists. It was true again with Picasso and to a certain extent with Matisse and Miró.

There is a similar reason, I think, behind the recent interest in sculpture by so many painters. Jackson Pollock, who had started out wanting to be a sculptor, pioneered a new kind of painting, the most distinctive characteristic of which is the way the materials themselves are handled. His drippings resulted in a continuous physicality of paint covering the entire surface, which created a new directness and immediacy. Color, light and dark, and pictorial space are integral to this paint covering; they exist as the inevitable physical consequence of applying paint to the surface. Often this continuous, literal flatness also led to all-over composition, a presiding evenness of pictorial pressure over the entire surface. As we have seen, all this put

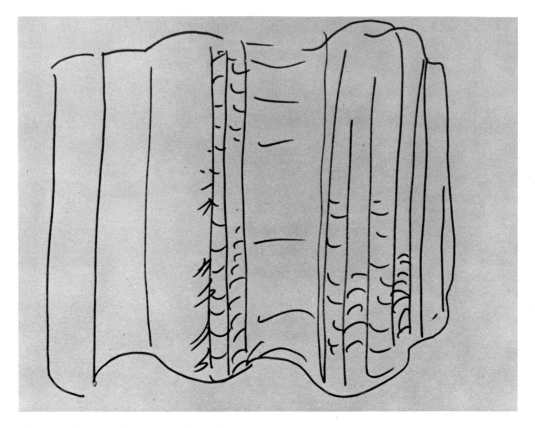

198. *Sculpture Sketch No. 7.* 1972.
Black felt-tip pen on blue textured paper, 8 7/8 × 11 7/8".
Collection of the artist

enormous pressure on contour or profile drawing, on inscribing shapes and forms (just the way that previous developments in painting put pressure on sculptural modeling). Forms in the older sense tend to break the literal immediacy and continuity of the surface, and, as Olitski's art demonstrates, all-overness works to push profile drawing to the very edges of the picture. Hence the popularity of the shaped canvas over the past fifteen years. Hence, too, the phenomenon of Minimal art. The Minimalists sought a literal directness and immediacy by fashioning three-dimensional works of simple shape that retain a pictorial-optical illusionism. The latter abstracts literalness through the use of the pictorial qualities of line and plane; at the same time illusionism becomes matter-of-fact illusionism, based on reality rather than on depiction and allusion.

Minimalist work does have an initial impact and an aggressive occupancy of space. It managed a new cleanness of contour and surface, and also something of the weightiness and density which are so much a part of traditional sculpture (but which abstract constructed sculpture has eschewed). But in real space, notions of wholeness and literalness derived from painting offer little more than arbitrary self-limitations. The requirements of singleness and simplicity radically limit and narrow an art based almost exclusively, as is Minimalism, on expressive shapes. And as one can see in recent Minimalist works, size and variation of material become the only areas left open to artistic discovery. The Minimalists were unwilling to engage three-dimensional issues. Frustrated by painting's suppression of drawing, they contented themselves with translating the wholeness and the literalness, the seeming blankness, of the new painting into real space. But literalness, all-overness, repetition, symmetry, and wholeness belong to abstract painting, where they function as a means of permitting other kinds of things, for example, broad chromatic effects, to emerge. They allow and encourage *pictorial* variation and development. In three dimensions they severely limit those very features—contour drawing, shape, composition—that contemporary sculpture is, or can be, all about.

Although a number of the color abstractionists have begun making sculpture, it is significant that none of them has shown much interest in "primary structures," or "specific objects," that is, Minimal art. All have made abstract, constructed sculpture related in one way or another to the tradition established by Picasso and González, and carried on by the work of David Smith and Anthony Caro. Another interesting difference is that Olitski, Noland, and others, unlike the Minimalists, do not see their three-dimensional work as something they do instead of painting or as an advance over their painting, but only (in the same way as Degas and Matisse before them) as an alternative and perhaps complementary activity.[1]

There is also a second and equally important reason for the recent turn to sculpture by abstract painters. The paintings of Pollock, and those of the next generation, especially Olitski and Noland, eliminated or made fully self-conscious the last assumptions of traditional easel painting. Henceforth, all limitations were to be self-limitations and transparent to the artists. One might expect that this new consciousness would lead to Alexandrianism or academicism. It may also do just this, but for the moment it has released the painter to interact with his materials and the issues of his medium in a freer way. He begins not with a prioris, but with the process of painting itself.

The lesson of Pollock's art was that abstract painting now had to do with finding new ways to combine paint and canvas so that both an illusion and a literal and continuous flatness

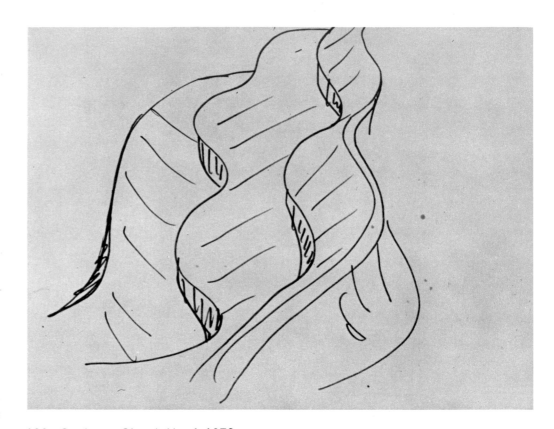

199. *Sculpture Sketch No. 4.* 1972.
Black felt-tip pen on pink textured paper, 8 7/8 × 11 7/8".
Collection of the artist

were created all at once. The rest of the picture—its composition, its image, its content, its form—was to be the result of the newly discovered way to apply paint, Pollock's highly unconventional technique of dripping and pouring pigments on a canvas laid out on the floor. The painter now had to keep himself open to possibilities inherent in the materials. He had to consciously avoid assumptions, a prioris. He began, not with forms—geometric or biomorphic—or even a certain kind of stroke, but simply with paint and canvas loosely or broadly conceived of as the materials. The process of painting had to be approached experimentally since this was where creativity now lay.

All genuinely new painting since Pollock has adopted these premises. Time and again, new ways of working with the materials, of combining paint and canvas, have led to new color, new layouts, a whole new feeling. Helen Frankenthaler, Morris Louis, Kenneth Noland, and Friedel Dzubas worked out multiple implications of staining, while Olitski discovered spraying and then explored what that implied. The same is true of Larry Poons' pouring. In each case, what is usually accounted "form" results from what is usually accounted "technique." For its part, technique—or more generally the materials—is elevated to what in older art was accounted the subject matter in the sense of that which provides both the challenge and resistance to the artist's invention and feeling.

All this had its effect on sculpture too, and, more specifically, on the work of Anthony Caro (pl. 150). Caro's renovation of abstract sculpture has often been described, but what has not yet been sufficiently stressed, I think, is that his contact with Noland and other Pollock-influenced figures provided the basis for his innovations. What lies behind these innovations is the conscious effort to work without a prioris, to let one's interaction with the materials lead to and ultimately determine the final result. Like Pollock in painting, Caro eliminated or made fully self-conscious the last conventions of traditional sculpture, that is, the last a prioris. And, as with painting, the result has been not a purified or reduced essence (as it had been for Brancusi and again for Minimalism) but an open approach to the medium, a programmatic effort to avoid one's own expectations and good taste, a conscious effort to devise and force creativity. Instead of a narrowing or a cul de sac or an absolute limit, multiple possibilities now opened up in both media—or so it seems. And the approach in both is similar.[2]

Paradoxically, this open, experimental approach to materials means that traditional technique and craft now play a *lesser* role. In any case, too great a fidelity to any one way of working can be inhibiting. Some of the solutions, say Larry Poons' pourings or Noland's taped bands, owe almost nothing to traditional procedures. This is also true of the new constructed sculpture, only more so. Older techniques—modeling, carving—have become totally irrelevant. Expression comes from choosing and then placing separate preexistent (or prefashioned) elements. The work does not bear the mark of the individual artist's handling. "Sensibility" becomes a question of the choice of materials, of intervals, thicknesses, widths, proportions, placements, joinings—choices which do not necessarily involve direct manipulation with the hands or fingers.[3] Even the joinings, such as bolting or welding, can be done by assistants. The work can be created in its entirety without the sculptor touching it at all (which, as we have seen, is the way Olitski's sculptures are made). From the first, this was implied by the very nature of constructed sculpture (and collage), but interestingly, the best and most important constructed sculpture—that of González, Picasso, and David Smith—continued

200. *Sculpture Drawing—December 1973—#1.* 1973.
Black wax crayon on paper, 11 × 13 7/8".
Collection of the artist

to have a handcrafted feeling. It was the Russian Constructivists, especially Gabo, who, though they were far less creative as sculptors, were first to accept the non-craft implications of construction.[4] Not until Anthony Caro, who was influenced by the open attitude toward art making of American painters like Noland (who in turn had been influenced by the open procedures of David Smith) on the one hand, and the English-European tradition of Constructivism on the other, were these non-craft implications made explicit and available to sculpture generally. They were clear enough in Caro's first large, brightly painted steel sculptures of the early 1960s. And they were further dramatized by Minimal sculpture, much of which was set forth in drawings and then industrially fabricated.

Today, painters are as much as ever involved with the "cookery" of painting: the amount of medium, glazing, admixtures, etc., as well as the way the paint is applied. In fact, invention is largely if not entirely located in these areas. However unorthodox, experimental, and open they are in approaching these aspects of painting, the art of painting itself is still craftlike. But this is no longer the case with contemporary sculpture, at least with the most dominant kind—abstract constructions. If contemporary sculpture is economically and physically more demanding to make than painting, it is, or can be, far less technically demanding or involving. Here sensibility and originality no longer lie in craft procedures. This less direct involvement with the more explicit character of the medium may actually make sculpture more difficult to conceive. But it certainly makes it easier for mature contemporary abstract painters to turn to sculpture (though not, it should be observed, the other way around). As a result, the sculpture done by contemporary abstract painters is by and large more ambitious than the sculpture done by earlier modernist painters.

It now rivals and challenges in scope and size the work of full-time sculptors, even though it is often done only on an occasional basis. On the other hand, like all painters' sculpture, it tends to remain pictorial and somewhat apart from uniquely sculptural issues; and full-time sculptors take as long to develop today as do painters.[5]

I am suggesting that it is precisely because modernist painting has consistently tended to force out or reduce the sculptural, that so many modern painters have been drawn to sculpture. In the most recent stage of this process, contour drawing and composition have been given a secondary place in most advanced abstract painting. Conveniently, contemporary abstract sculpture is primarily about these very things.

Despite all predictions, abstract sculpture has remained the secondary visual art in the twentieth century. Until recently, perhaps only Brancusi and Lipchitz, Picasso and González, and then David Smith and Anthony Caro have been able to achieve works which equal in quality and originality the very best of abstract painting produced in this century. While its development has its own internal consistency and logic, abstract sculpture has not been able to sustain momentum. Most often it has relied on painting for periodic transfusions. This was true for Picasso, for David Smith, and for the early works of Anthony Caro. It is particularly true at the moment. If sculpture today seems to be growing in vigor it is in part thanks to painting.

At first it seems odd that painters should have been the first to reach a completely open attitude toward their processes and materials. Sculptors had looked to their materials as the basis of art-making earlier in this century, but they too were prompted by collage and developments in painting. And the emphasis on materials and the possibilities they offered was for Gabo, Boccioni, and others more a question of theory than

201. *Sculpture Drawing—July 1974—#5*. 1974.
Black felt-tip pen on paper, 17 3/4 × 11 7/8".
Collection of the artist

practice and pretty much confined to the idea of *new* materials. Their attitudes towards working itself were less radical. Also, like Picasso, they seemed to lack the confidence or vision to work out the implications of their own insights or intimations. Sculptors had to wait for painters to show the way; and painters still had more conventions of representational art to creatively eliminate or become aware of. Sculpture continued to be defined in terms of truth to specific craft procedures, especially carving, or in terms of a mystique of materials. Sculptors sought a kind of essence of procedures: "truth to materials," "direct carving," or art defined in terms of one specific expressive feature such as shape or volume or space. Sculptors tended to be reductionist just as were so many abstract painters before 1950. It is no accident that Picasso, González, and David Smith, the real bearers of the future in abstract sculpture, did not think this way. As if to avoid premature innovation, they retained certain representational conventions and remained loosely oriented to images drawn from the real world, usually a figure.

The fact that sculpture is harder to isolate or define than painting may help explain its insecurity. The basic, irreducible conventions of sculpture turn out, surprisingly enough, to be less specific and less literal than those of painting. Painting is identified by its flat surface and its enclosing shape, but sculpture cannot be pinned so explicitly. In the modernist context, with its bias toward explicitness, this lack of specific identity has meant insecurity. The modern sculptor has been fearful of producing an arbitrary object or a work that looks utilitarian. More recently this lack of clear self-definition has meant a lack of firm resistance or coordinates against which to work.

Clement Greenberg has said that sculpture is the most "representative" modernist art. By this he meant that it fulfills "our modern taste for the literal, positive, irreducible."[6] I would say that it is representative in still another, perhaps even more essential sense; it fulfills our modern individualistic artists' dream of creating a totally new, totally autonomous, and totally personal unity—a completely new object in the world, purely creative. Being confined to two dimensions, the painter's unity is more abstract, but it is an abstract unity based on concrete, literal limits. The condition itself of sculpture is literally concrete, but its coordinates are abstract and undefined. One might think that without these limits, sculpture would be freer or more open-ended and more able to create radically new unities. Though this may prove to be the case in the long run, it has not been the case so far. Perhaps this is due to that lack of concrete limits which give a sense of resistance, of friction, of feedback, of something to work away from, or toward, of a place to begin. Lacking this self-definition, this "essence," or at least such definite and palpable coordinates, sculpture has been less radical, or less consistently radical. If a lack of givens makes abstract sculpture potentially freer and more autonomous, it also makes the invention of new forms more difficult and creates a dependency on painting, to which sculpture has turned again and again for orientation.

Related to this is the fact that abstract constructed sculpture does not depend on traditional sculpture in the way that the abstract picture depends for its identity on traditional easel painting. It differs far more from traditional sculpture than abstract painting does from traditional painting. This also produces insecurity. Constructed sculpture is more like a qualitatively new medium; it is not the product of an essentializing process but rather is a hybrid. It involves making three-dimensional work with two-dimensional elements. The reason it has had to confine itself to two-dimensional elements has to

202. *Sculpture Sketch—August 22, 1974—#1.* 1974.
Colored oil pastels on paper, 9 3/8 × 14 3/8".
Collection of the artist

do with what I have elsewhere called "the problem of section," the inability of sculpture to give a sense of section, of inside, of mass-filling or enclosed volume, without portraying animate beings.[7] If this interpretation is correct, modernist sculpture's limitation to two-dimensional elements is not temporary.[8] But in any event, this limitation has certainly prevailed until now, and together with the other points mentioned above helps to explain why modernist sculpture continues to be so bound up with modernist painting.

As significant as painters' sculpture has been since the mid-nineteenth century, until recently it has tended to lack real ambition and authority. Degas and Matisse, and to a lesser extent Daumier and Renoir, were certainly important sculptors, but their sculpture remains relatively traditional and modest (in Degas' case even private). Matisse's sculpture, as good as it is, doesn't add up to an independent body of work. Even Picasso, who gave constructivist sculpture its start, didn't really carry through with it. But one can hardly imagine a purer painter, a more painterly painter, than Olitski. Yet his sculpture is as ambitious and as innovative and as followed-through as that of any sculptor working today. His sculptural and draughtsmanly gifts and impulses seem to be almost as much there as his purely painterly ones. But the state of painting and sculpture in our time does not permit the realization of all these gifts in the same medium.[9]

It is instructive to think of Olitski's sculpture together with that of one other American sculptor, Michael Steiner, whose work also had its immediate origin in painting.[10] Beginning as a painter of shaped canvases and then working for a while as a Minimalist, Steiner finally began making constructed sculpture in the late '60s. In his large steel pieces, he has found a way to exploit Minimalism's rigid, schematic drawing by setting it against matter, as it were (pl. 204). Very abstract in feeling, this mode allows him to use large planes that have an effective breadth and, especially, thickness; he can thus be inventive in three dimensions while achieving a feeling of density new to abstract constructed sculpture. In fact, it could be said that by bearing down so hard on the dimension of *thickness* (of his parts), by giving as much expressive weight to it as to width and length, Steiner was the first to make constructed steel sculpture so fully three-dimensional (David Smith's "Cubi" sculptures were his only precedent).

Olitski did not come out of Minimalism. In fact, it was his holistic paintings of 1962 and 1963 that influenced Minimalism in the first place. He is also interested in something quite different. Like Steiner, he wants to make original constructed sculpture rather than to try to eliminate sculptural interest for the sake of some kind of objecthood.[11]

He begins with an a priori conception, either a given gestalt like the rings or a broad idea like the ones projected in his drawings and collages. The materials are handled loosely—in a casual or seemingly accidental way. If Steiner sets taut, schematic line against matter, Olitski sets a loose linear idea (but in rigid steel) against its relaxed, "dumb" realization. Both exploit the sharp distance between conception and realization that is potentially present in modern sculpture. Steiner uses this distance to expand the period of conception, to permit himself to conceive his pieces in a manageable material like plywood, and then he has the result fabricated in steel. Olitski contracts the period of conception. He projects graphic ideas and then lets a looser, less controlled act of making take over as his sensibility or "touch." Steiner begins with individual pieces, or a spatial idea, not a graphic conception. For him sensibility lies in a found idea and then in his strict control of all the

203. David Smith. *Zig IV July 7—1961*. 1961.
Painted steel, 94 7/8 × 76 1/2".
Lincoln Center for the Performing Arts, Inc., New York

204. Michael Steiner. *Knossos.* 1972.
Cor-ten steel, 56 × 108 × 92".
Collection Lois and Georges de Menil, Paris, France

dimensions. Of course, Steiner is interested in sculptural issues that go all the way back to Polyclitus: axis and balance, felt internal structure, real vs. apparent weight or support, tension and relaxation, etc. From this point of view, Olitski's sculpture remains pictorial, a painter's sculpture. But taken together, Steiner and Olitski might be seen as an American alternative to the Caro school, which, with its origin in European collage and Constructivism, has tended to be inspired by individual, given, and often found parts and the joining of these discontinuous parts. The results have usually been a light, weightless, very open kind of pictorialism. The varied vocabulary keeps the emphasis on axes and vectors. And even Caro's best large pieces, such as *Fathom*, are open and light in feeling when compared to the American work. The individual pieces still tend to be conspicuous and the whole has an expressive lightness. (Some of Caro's recent work may have been influenced by American sculpture both in its emphasis on contour drawing and in his moves toward a "weighted" monumentalism, although the latter might have very possibly occurred in any event.)

The American sculptors have been influenced not only by the working attitudes of recent American painting but also by its form. They employ a more or less uniform vocabulary of broad, rectangular, dark sheets of steel that places the expressive emphasis on plane, edge, thickness—on drawing as line—and on materiality and physicality. Their sculpture thus appropriates an area all to itself, and is seemingly less open, more holistic, like one coherent thing with its own density and potential monumentality. Once again modernist painting has given a fresh stimulus to modernist sculpture, and this stimulus, paradoxically, now permits modernist sculpture to reclaim many features associated with traditional sculpture.

WORKS IN CLAY

205. *Brown Slab One*. 1975.
Stoneware with colored slips, 23 × 16''.
Collection of the artist

206. *Brown Slab Two*. 1975.
Stoneware with colored slips, 30 × 13 1/2''.
Collection of the artist

207. *First Yav*. 1975. Stoneware, 36 × 33 × 24″. Collection of the artist

208. *Second Yav*. 1975.
Stoneware, 37 × 33 × 24″.
Collection of the artist

209. *Cool Satin 0*. 1975. Glazed stoneware, 8 × 40 × 41″. Collection of the artist

210. *Iron Cone 02–3*. 1975. Stoneware, 12 × 120 × 84″. Collection of the artist

NOTES TO CHAPTER FOUR

1. The Minimalists led the way here even if they missed the point; and they undoubtedly had some influence on serious sculpture. But hemmed in by the narrowness of their own conception, Minimalist sculptors themselves have hardly been able to develop at all since their emergence in the mid-1960s. As we have seen, scale, size, and material were the only areas left open to them. But sculpture offers the possibility of working with shape and relationships in space. Maybe it was out of frustration with Minimalism that many young artists were driven to project "primary forms" into nature (earth works), or were driven back to painting, where, given Minimalism's self-limitations, there was more room for variation, if not for real artistic development. Minimalism can no longer claim to transcend painting. By now it is clear that Minimalism is a period look or mode common to both mediums; and it is a look which had its origin and raison d'être in abstract painting.

2. In both mediums, for example, artists now add so that they can take away. When painting, Olitski often works on a large canvas tacked to the floor, from which he later crops a picture or pictures. Similarly, in his sculptures, he can stack up many elements, try to "see" a sculpture in the pile, and edit it out. In both cases, the artist sees an advantage in avoiding preconceptions at the beginning so as to leave things open to discovery later.

3. The sculpture of Mark di Suvero is a perfect lesson here. Di Suvero undermines what are sometimes interesting sculptural ideas by not dealing with these features. It may be that this is a result of overstressing gesture a la Abstract Expressionism, or, more simply, because he aims at a tough, difficult, or outrageous look.

4. A central problem in the history of modern art is why it took so long for constructed sculpture to develop. Even Picasso, who invented it, left it for almost twenty years before taking it up again, only to drop it again after a few years. Gabo is also an interesting case in this regard, since he grasped many of the inherent tendencies of constructed sculpture but was unable to turn this insight into important art—at least in a sustained way. The kind of emphasis on materials, transparency, and weightlessness he achieved was usually too literal, almost representational (suspending a sculpture from the ceiling, using transparent plexiglass, etc.), not integrally abstract or truly sculptural.

5. Clement Greenberg has remarked how painters' sculpture tends to fall outside the development of sculpture except in the epochal and monumental case of Picasso.

6. Clement Greenberg, "The New Sculpture," in *Art and Culture*, Boston, Beacon Press, 1961, pp. 143–44.

7. See my catalogue, *Michael Steiner*, Boston, Museum of Fine Arts, 1974. I note there my debt to Terry Fenton in relation to my idea of the "problem of section."

8. Since it deals with real, literal elements and without the abstracting that automatically results from the flat picture plane, abstract sculpture needs to be more abstract in form. This is the reason why geometry and/or clean, faired, and trued edges impose themselves more on abstract sculpture than on abstract painting. For all its pictorialism, the new sculpture tends to be non-painterly, or, better, "linear" in Wölfflin's sense of the term. Olitski's new sculpture, however, does manage to get a rich, chiaroscuro painterliness into abstract, constructed sculpture.

9. From this point of view, it is interesting to think of Olitski's life drawings (pls. 138–43). See *Jules Olitski: Life Drawings*, introduction by Andrew Hudson, Washington, D.C., Corcoran Gallery of Art, 1971. In the medium of drawing he is representational—something he cannot be in either his painting or sculpture. It is as if Olitski seeks to retain, and if possible revive, all of tradition, but only insofar as his modernism allows. In this respect he is similar to Picasso, who also found a modernist outlet for his many gifts and impulses by dividing himself, working in different styles or using different styles for different media.

Andrew Hudson, in his catalogue to Olitski's life drawings, points out that Olitski began these drawings at about the same time as the beginning of his spray paintings. But, of course, he had always drawn:

". . . Olitski talked to me of his life-long interest in drawing. As a child, he learned to draw almost at the same time that he learned to read, and drew from photographs in the newspaper; as a teenager, he won a scholarship to study drawing at the Pratt Institute; and he has kept on drawing ever since, despite a few lapses of some years. When teaching at Bennington College, he asked to change the school policy and have nude models, and he emphasized drawing in his teaching (along with working from nature and looking at the Old Masters). Later, when visiting Bennington after he had quit his teaching job, he would drop in to draw with the students in the evening life classes. And in recent years in New York, he has belonged to various drawing groups organized around one or two friends."

Hudson continues:

"He described to me how, just as in portraiture, the essential thing in drawing is a certain relationship with the model. If that's there, he said, the drawings come out better than they would normally; if it's not, you can do technically correct drawing but it will be lifeless. If the feeling is there, you feel "connected" and even if the drawing isn't correct, it still has some living quality; at times a kind of intensity takes place that almost assures good drawing . . ."

10. There are several interesting parallels and differences between these two artists. Many of Steiner's early constructions have the look of shaped reliefs. Olitski's ring pieces, on the other hand, are far more painting-like than relief-like.

11. See Michael Fried, "Art and Objecthood," in *Minimal Art,* Gregory Battcock, ed., New York, E. P. Dutton, 1968.

211. Olitski's house at South Shaftsbury, Vt. 1964. Sculpture by Anthony Caro

CHRONOLOGY*
BY ELINOR L. WORON AND KENWORTH MOFFETT

1922 Born March 27 in Snovsk, Russia, the only child of Jevel and Anna Demikovsky (née Zarnitsky). His father, a commissar, is executed by the Soviet government in 1921, a few months before Olitski's birth. The family subsequently moves to Gomel.

1923 Emigrates in August with mother and grandmother to the United States. Lives in Jamaica, New York, for a few months at the home of his uncle Nathan Zarnin, whose financial assistance and sponsorship made their emigration possible. Moves from there to Sackman Street, Brooklyn. Mother works to support family.

1926–40 Mother marries Hyman Olitsky (1926), a widower with two sons, Sidney and Bernard. Half-sister Rosalyn Olitsky is born. Family remains in Brooklyn, then moves to Patchogue, Long Island, where Jules attends elementary school. They return to Brooklyn, where he attends Winthrop Junior High School (1934–37) and Samuel J. Tilden High School (1937–40). Although there is no interest in art in his family, Olitski shows particular enthusiasm and talent for drawing.

1935 Death of maternal grandmother, Freida Zarnitsky, is, a traumatic experience for Olitski, who begins to question the meaning of his own life and focus more strongly on his desire to become an artist. Briefly attends children's art

classes on Saturday mornings in New York City, where Chaim Gross, Sol Wilson, Moses Soyer, and Raphael Soyer are among the instructors. Olitski remembers working in plaster and wood.

1939 Sees paintings and African sculptures at the Brooklyn Museum. Then is very affected by

213. High school graduation photo

212. United States Passport Photo of Jules Olitski and his mother Anne. c. 1923

seeing Rembrandt portraits for the first time on a visit to the New York World's Fair. He begins visiting museums around New York City, returning often to look at the Sargent watercolors in the Brooklyn Museum.

Wins scholarship prize offered by a department store to study drawing at the Pratt Institute. He remembers working there once a week in charcoal for three months perfecting the drawing of an antique portrait bust. After finishing, he leaves Pratt.

1940 Meets Impressionist-style painter Samuel Rothbort during installation of this artist's exhibition at Tilden High School. Rothbort invites Olitski to paint with him outdoors around Sheepshead Bay. He works in oils for the first

---

*In this chronology we have made use of information provided by Jules Olitski, Dawn Andrews, Howard Conant, Michael Freilich, Sidney Geist, Clement Greenberg, Seymour Hacker, and Pierre Matisse, and by the following galleries: André Emmerich, David Mirvish, Poindexter, and Lawrence Rubin.

time, painting landscapes, scenes of the docks, and boats in the water.

Awarded art prize at high school graduation. Head of art department, Herbert Yates, encourages Olitski to continue his study of painting with a view toward becoming an art teacher.

1940–42 After graduating from high school, he is admitted to the National Academy of Design, New York, where he studies life drawing and portrait painting with Sidney Dickinson, a prom-

215. Olitski at the National Academy of Design, New York. c. 1940

inent portraitist and National Academician. In the evenings, he studies sculpture at the Beaux Arts Institute, where he works figuratively, mostly in clay.

First encounter with totally abstract art is at the Museum of Non-Objective Painting (later named the Solomon R. Guggenheim Museum), then under the direction of Hilla Rebay. He especially remembers paintings by Kandinsky and Bauer. This experience does not influence his style at this time, however.

1942 Meets painter Victor Thall, who had been living in Paris and taught at the Art Students League. A small group of young painters meets in Thall's New York apartment and submits paintings for criticism. For a time, Olitski is part of this group. With Thall, he frequently visits the Museum of Modern Art and the Metropolitan Museum of Art where he becomes interested in works by Cézanne, Manet, and the Impressionists, as well as paintings by Matisse, Vlaminck, Derain, and the Nabis, Bonnard and Vuillard. Under Thall's influence he begins to use color more freely in a somewhat Fauvist manner.

1942–45 He is drafted into the United States Army. While in the army, he becomes a United States citizen and legally takes his stepfather's name, Olitsky. He studies at Purdue University under the auspices of the Army Specialized Training Program. Marries Gladys Katz.

1945–48 Upon discharge from the army, Olitski lives in Brooklyn for a short time. Moves to Asheville, North Carolina, for a year, where he is attracted by the local landscape. Hitchhikes with wife to Mexico, planning to spend a year painting in a fishing village, but finds the landscape and effect of sunlight too excessive and dramatic. Illness and medical expenses drain his resources, and after approximately a month, Olitski returns to New York, where he lives on Henry Street on the lower East Side of Manhattan. He also lives for a time in Sheepshead Bay, Brooklyn. Continues to paint Fauve-like pictures, but simultaneously uses a Rembrandt-esque, chiaroscuro style in his portraits.

214. Sidney Dickinson's class at the National Academy of Design, New York (Olitski in back at right). c. 1940

216. Olitski at 18 with self-portrait

217. Olitski at Chaim Gross' studio (Gross in back at right). 1947

Studies sculpture at the Educational Alliance with Chaim Gross (1947) and does clay and plaster semi-abstract, figurative sculptures. Also does stone and wood carvings. Uncertain whether he will become a sculptor or a painter.

Daughter Eve is born (July 1948).

1949–51 Aided by the G. I. Bill, Olitski travels to Paris. Studies with the sculptor Ossip Zadkine for a few months, then enrolls at the Académie de la Grande Chaumière, where he remains registered for a year, but does not attend classes. Does semi-abstract plaster reliefs, but after leaving Zadkine's studio he concentrates completely on painting. He has a studio outside Paris in Chaville and later in Paris, on Rue des Suisses, near the Métro station Plaisance.

His interest in Jean Dubuffet is aroused by reading an essay by the American critic Clement Greenberg, "School of Paris, 1946," and Olitski goes to see Dubuffet's paintings at Galerie Rive Gauche. Michel Tapié shows him paintings by Dubuffet which Olitski later described as "all-over impasto" type pictures. According to him, this experience influenced his later impasto paintings from the end of the 1950s. He also sees works by Bonnard and Braque at Galerie Maeght and paintings by Picasso and Gris at Daniel-Henry Kahnweiler's Galerie Louise Leiris.

Despite these artistic contacts, Olitski says for the most part he isolated himself from his artistic surroundings. He stayed away from museums, including the Louvre, and he remained uninvolved with current European trends. Olitski describes these Paris years as an "introspective" time of his life; he was questioning his own identity as a painter and straining to break away from his academic training. "At the time, I thought that my art had very little to do with

218. Olitski in Paris with a picture (now destroyed) that was shown at Galerie Huit. 1951

what I was about, and establishing some contact with myself was the problem that began to occupy me. . . . I had to look inside, but how do you not look out? Then I did the curious and simple-minded thing: I wrapped something around my eyes and began to dab at the canvas and every now and then I would permit myself to peek at what was happening. I did this for a number of months, and the result was a series of flat, abstract paintings which seemed very alive to me. This was my backwards way of becoming involved with abstract art." (From an interview with Donna Poydinecz-Conley, Summer 1978; typescript in Olitski's possession.)

Obviously Olitski wants to break with academic style and free himself from everything he has known and learned to do with ease. By painting with a blindfold on, then removing it to consciously reinforce forms and confirm images, he is able to overcome his own facility. These paintings are loosely painted with flat areas of bright color and Surrealist automatic painting. The imagery is bestial, scatological, and nightmarish. They remind one of Picasso and of the pictures that were being done by the European group CoBrA at that time.

1950 Meets sculptor Sidney Geist, a member of a cooperative group of young American artists

who start Galerie Huit on Rue St. Julien le Pauvre. Organized by Tajiri Shinkichi, the group also includes Oscar Chelemsky, John Anderson, Larry Calcagno, Al Held, Rudolph Baranik, Reginald Pollack, and Burton Hasen. The gallery had previously been the studio of sculptor Robert Rosenwald, who was leaving Paris and offered the space to them rent-free for a period of time.

Participates in "Americans in Paris Exhibition" at Hacker Gallery, New York (Dec. 5–30). Exhibition is organized by Sidney Geist and includes works by Tajiri Shinkichi, George Ortman, Gabriel Cohen, and Sidney Geist. Carlyle Burrows (*Herald Tribune,* Dec. 10, 1950) writes that Olitski's "paintings have a savage vigor that marks the work with both intelligence and strong feeling."

1951 Olitski's first one-artist show is held at Galerie Huit. He exhibits semi-abstract paintings executed in bright, spectral colors that developed out of the blindfold works. He is approached by CoBrA painters Constant, Appel, and Corneille. They ask him to exhibit with them, but personal problems force him to leave Europe and return to New York. Divorced from wife.

1952–54 Earns B.S. degree in art education at New York University. Works part-time as assistant in Department of Art Education at New York University (1953–56).

Reacts against intense, aggressive colors and imagery of Paris works. Paints monochromatic pictures using drawing boards as models, in which the central field or plane remains empty and the painterly incident is pushed to the margins of the picture. The configuration presages Olitski's post-1964 work.

First work exhibited in New York is shown at Roko Gallery in group exhibition organized by

Michael Freilich (June 1953). Others participating are Louise Nevelson, William King, Robert Andrew Parker, Walter Williams, and Alex Katz. Freilich describes Olitski's works of this time as landscape in feeling but moving toward a personal kind of abstraction.

Occasionally exhibits work in jury-selected group shows at City Center Art Gallery (1954).

Joins faculty as assistant professor of art, Department of Art Education, State University College at New Paltz, New York (Sept. 1954– June 1955).

1955 Earns M.A. degree at New York University. Works toward doctoral degree. Serves as curator of the New York University Art Education Gallery until 1956. Organizes exhibitions of "Contemporary Indonesian Paintings," "Paintings by Neuro-Psychiatric Patients," and "Photography," among others. Also organizes a series of panel discussions held at the gallery. During the 1950s, Olitski sometimes visits the Iolas Gallery, the Matisse Gallery, the Kootz Gallery (where he remembers seeing the works of Hans Hofmann), the Egan Gallery, and he remembers seeing at least one Pollock exhibition at the Janis Gallery.

1956 Marries Andrea Hill Pearce. After living in Brooklyn for a short time, they move to East Norwich, Long Island (1958), then to Northport, Long Island. Daughter Lauren is born (March 1957).

Joins faculty at C. W. Post College of Long Island University, Greenvale, New York, where he becomes associate professor and chairman of the Fine Arts Department, remaining until 1963.

1958 First one-man show in the United States is an exhibition of heavily impastoed paintings at Zodiac Gallery, a small room set aside at Iolas Gallery in which works of new artists are shown. Catalogue prints his name with the European spelling, "Olitski"; he prefers this spelling and retains it. Clement Greenberg sees the exhibition and is interested in Olitski's paintings. Olitski meets Greenberg at this time, and Greenberg becomes a close friend whose encouragement and criticism have been centrally important for Olitski ever since.

Greenberg becomes consultant to French & Co. Invites Olitski to be represented by the gallery and to participate in a group show in December along with Friedel Dzubas, Adolph Gottlieb, Wolfgang Hollegha, Morris Louis, Barnett Newman, Kenneth Noland, and David Smith.

1959 One-man exhibition at French & Co. in May of impasto paintings in which spackle, paint, colored pigments, and acrylic resins are employed. The works are executed in subtle, neutral tonalities. They suggest nonobjective bas-reliefs to Stuart Preston (*New York Times*, May 24, 1959), who feels Olitski's work occupies a territory between painting and sculpture.

Barbara Rose (*Artforum*, Sept. 1965) writes that "Olitski's paintings [of this period] which, in their insistence on matter and texture, seem to have something to do with European 'art informel,' are possibly the oddest paintings done by any American of his generation. But their renunciation of space behind the frame in favor of an almost exclusively tactile involvement with a relief-like building up on top of the surface might also be seen as the acknowledgment of the contradictions in either Abstract Expressionist or 'informal' painting."

219. Olitski with Anthony Caro and Kenneth Noland in Shaftesbury, Vt. Early 1960s

The exhibition consists of twenty-six paintings, including *Moliere's Chair II*. During installation, Olitski meets Kenneth Noland, who helps him to hang the show.

1960 Important change in style. Begins to pour and stain dye onto larger canvases, creating sharp-edged, irregular areas of intense color on a matte black ground. Sense of texture and impasto is eliminated. Technical problems inherent in the medium, however, cause Olitski to overpaint these works with enamel. Only a few paintings of this period still exist.

1961 Second one-artist show at French & Co. (Apr. 20–May 14) with seventeen dye paintings. French & Co. closes its contemporary painting department, and Elinor Poindexter asks him to join her gallery, where he exhibits in October and every succeeding year through 1965.

Osculum Silence (1960), a dye picture, wins second prize for painting ($1,500) at the Pittsburgh International Exhibition of Contemporary Painting and Sculpture, sponsored by the Carnegie Institute (Oct. 27, 1961–Jan. 7, 1962). Award jury includes Lawrence Alloway, Robert Giron, Seymour Knox, Kenzo Okada, and Daniel Catton Rich. The exhibition has 524 paintings and sculptures. First prize is awarded to Mark Tobey (*Untitled*); third prize, Adolph Gottlieb (*Tan Over Black*); fourth prize, Ellsworth Kelly (*Block Island No. 2*); fifth prize, Wolfgang Hollegha (*Bird*). *Osculum Silence* is given by G. David Thompson to The Museum of Modern Art, New York.

1962 Olitski is invited to exhibit in Italy by the dealer Toninelli. Works on a series of pictures subsequently called the "Italian Paintings" because they are exhibited in Florence, Rome, and Milan. These are hard-edge works in which precisely drawn elliptical forms are executed in intense colors. In an effort to get away from the opacity of the dye works, Olitski experiments with homemade, water-based acrylic, similar to Liquitex, applied to the canvas with a brush and sponge. He then changes to the technique of staining thinned Magna acrylic into unprimed canvas with sponges, brushes, and occasionally rollers. (Olitski works with Magna until his first big spray painting of 1964, when the smell and fumes that result from spraying Magna "drove him out of the studio" and prompted him to use water-soluble acrylics, which he has used ever since. Magna is turpentine-soluble.)

Paintings are organized around a central "core" of color or raw canvas, with alternating and irregular concentric bands of saturated color and ground expanding outward to intersect the framing edge. Major stain painting of this period, *Born in Snovsk*, is later purchased by the Ford Foundation and presented as a gift to the Art Institute of Chicago on March 18, 1964.

Clement Greenberg ("After Abstract Expressionism," *Art International*, Oct. 1962) remarks that the real chance taken with color in Jules Olitski's "pure" painting provokes shock among New York artists.

220. Olitski with his daughter, Lauren, at home in South Shaftesbury. c. 1964. Diamond painting by Kenneth Noland and an early experimental spray picture by Olitski (*Pizzazz.* 1963), at right

1963 Barbara Rose (*Art International*, Apr. 1963) writes: "Among Jules Olitski's new works are the best paintings shown this year in New York. . . . Olitski provides an infinite number of sophisticated variations, of color harmonies, of scale, of contour and of the possible relationships of parts. . . . Exceeding the limits of the canvas, the forms convey an expansiveness and largeness of conception that is like the way baroque forms overflow their boundaries."

Participates in "Three New American Painters: Louis, Noland, Olitski" at the Norman Mackenzie Art Gallery, University of Saskatchewan, Regina, Canada (Jan. 11–Feb. 15). The exhibition is organized by Clement Greenberg, at the request of Gerald Finley, acting director of the gallery. In his introduction to the catalogue Greenberg states: "Olitski was already exceptional when he was a portrait painter, and he remained so as the maker of thickly impastoed pictures in a European vein of abstraction, and more recently as an explorer of high-keyed combinations of very flat color. The work he showed over the last two years in New York was some of the most unconventional to be seen anywhere in American painting. Yet hardly anything he has done before matches the . . . present canvases in resolved strength or in clarity and harmony." From this exhibition the Norman Mackenzie Art Gallery purchases *Ino Delight.*

One-man exhibitions at Galleria Santacroce, Florence (Feb.), Galleria Topazia Alliata, Rome (Apr.), and Toninelli Arte Moderne, Milan (Sept.)

Teaches at Bennington College, Bennington, Vermont, from September 1963 until 1967. Lives in South Shaftsbury, Vermont.

1964 Begins to use eight-inch rollers of industrial type almost exclusively to apply water-base paint, rolling one color into another so that color changes take place within the paint flow. Color fills almost entire surface. Leaves the edges bare, asserting the flatness of the picture surface and the expansive qualities of color.

During a conversation in the spring with Noland and Anthony Caro, Olitski remarks that an ideal situation for him would be to spray color into the air and somehow have it remain there. In 1963, Olitski had already experimented briefly on small canvases with cans of spray paint bought in a hardware store, but had been dissatisfied with the results. Immediately after this conversation, however, he paints his first large spray painting, using spray gun and compressor.

The Museum of Modern Art, New York, exchanges *Osculum Silence* with Olitski for *Cleopatra Flesh* on April 14.

One-man exhibition at Kasmin Gallery, London in April. Subsequent exhibitions in 1965, 1968, 1969, 1970, 1972.

Selected by Clement Greenberg to participate in "Post Painterly Abstraction" at Los Angeles County Museum (Apr. 23–June 7), an exhibition conceived by the museum together with preceding exhibitions of Pop painting for the purpose of showing the two developments in recent American painting. Greenberg points out in his introduction to the catalogue that most of the works in the "Post Painterly Abstraction" exhibition are a reaction against the attitudes of painterly abstraction and have in common a trend toward openness and clarity, use of high-keyed, lucid colors, anonymous execution often through the use of geometric forms and the elimination of tactile paint handling.

In the summer, Olitski is invited to conduct the Emma Lake Workshop, organized by the Art Department, University of Saskatchewan, Regina. Among the others who have directed the workshop are Lawrence Alloway, Herman Cherry, Donald Judd, Clement Greenberg, Barnett Newman, Kenneth Noland, Frank Stella, and Michael Steiner. Olitski is the first artist to set up a studio and work there.

Works painted at this time are sometimes referred to as "curtain pictures," in which large, modulated fields of color are rolled and stained into raw canvas, spreading toward but not achieving the framing edge. These works, precursors of his spray paintings, are later exhibited in "Three American Painters," at the Fogg Art Museum, Cambridge, Massachusetts (1965).

Around this time Olitski begins to use chalk drawing on pictures as a framing device.

One-man exhibition at Galerie Lawrence, Paris (autumn).

One-man exhibition of paintings executed at Emma Lake Workshop, David Mirvish Gallery, Toronto (Dec. 12, 1964–Jan. 7, 1965). Subsequent shows at Mirvish in 1965, 1966, 1968, 1971, 1972, 1973, 1976.

1965 In the spring, Olitski begins to develop fully the technique of spray painting in which he draws a length of unprimed canvas through a trough of acrylic paint to saturate it. Placing wet canvas on the floor, he sprays it with pigment through spray guns, powered by an electric air compressor. Sometimes works with three guns at once, cutting back to one or two in order to create different densities of color. Later eliminates soaking process and simultaneous use of two guns. Works first with Magna acrylic but, because of the dangers of turpentine fumes, soon changes to water-base Aqua-tec. Also begins using a single spray gun with a variety of nozzles for greater control. In early spray paintings the edges are free of incident. Later, perimeters are defined with brushstrokes of paint, pastel, or crayon.

Rosalind Krauss discusses these paintings in her introduction to the catalogue *Jules Olitski: Recent Paintings* (Institute of Contemporary Art, University of Pennsylvania, 1968): "Jules Olitski first began to register his vision of open, undemarcated expanses of color by means of the spray technique. Even as he did so, his convictions about the role of color within the development of major abstract painting had coalesced into a deeply felt resolve . . . for Olitski, the spray medium became not only the most lucid means of expressing his own feelings about color, but a vehicle for challenging the limitations placed on color by the most radical of his contemporaries. Michael Fried (*Artforum,*

221. Olitski at the Venice Biennale. 1966

Nov. 1965) observes: "For modernism as well as neoclassicism, painting is not merely a gratification for the sight. It is a dialectical cognitive and (in the deep sense of the word) conventional enterprise which, in Jules Olitski's new paintings, has given us works to match the art of the museums in quality, conviction and—perhaps most astonishingly of all—naturalness."

First spray paintings shown at Poindexter Gallery, New York (Oct. 26–Nov. 13) and David Mirvish Gallery, Toronto (Nov. 11–Dec. 5).

At this time Michael Fried writes (*Artforum,* Nov. 1965): "[Olitski's paintings of the past nine or ten months] are, I believe, among the most beautiful, authoritative and moving creations of our time in any art. They differ from his own previous work in their complete freedom from anything that smacks of eccentricity, caprice

222. Olitski with Larry Poons. 1968

or artiness; and they are distinguished from paintings in deductive formats by their ease, sensuousness and accessibility."

Begins in the winter to mask edges of already sprayed canvas around two or three sides, then sprays again and removes masking. In this way, he gets both color and a stenciled echo of the framing edge. He moves away from narrow vertical format to square and horizontal shaped canvas.

Does a few sculptures of corrugated fiberglass and tin, which were spray painted (until 1967).

1966 Olitski is one of four painters selected by Henry Geldzahler to represent the United States in the "XXXIII International Biennial Exhibition of Art," Venice, organized by the Smithsonian Institution (June 18–Oct. 6). Other artists included are Helen Frankenthaler, Roy Lichtenstein, and Ellsworth Kelly. In the catalogue essay Clement Greenberg writes: "Olitski has turned out what I do not hesitate to call masterpieces in every phase of his art. The masterpieces do seem to increase in frequency as color is given more rein."

One-man exhibition at Nicholas Wilder Gallery, Los Angeles (June). Shows again at Wilder in 1973.

Begins in the fall to thicken sprayed paint by adding pure ammonia to the pigment. Introduces irregular margins of impastoed paint along one, two, or three sides to define framing edge of sprayed paintings. Some are shown in one-man exhibition at David Mirvish Gallery, Toronto (Oct. 15–Nov. 7).

One-man exhibition at André Emmerich Gallery, New York (Oct. 29–Nov. 17). Subsequent exhibitions at Emmerich in 1967, 1978.

1967 Wins first prize, $2,000, and a gold medal at the "30th Biennial Exhibition of Contemporary American Painting" at the Corcoran Gallery of Art, Washington, D.C. (Feb. 24–Apr. 19), for *Pink Alert*. Jury consists of three museum directors: Bartlett Hayes (Addison Gallery of American Art), Evan Turner (Philadelphia Museum of Art), and James Elliot (Wadsworth Atheneum). Other prizes go to Paul Jenkins, John McLaughlin, and Kenneth Noland. *Pink Alert* is purchased by the Friends of the Corcoran.

First one-man museum show, "Jules Olitski: Paintings 1963–1967," is held at the Corcoran Gallery of Art, Washington, D.C. (Apr.–May). Circulates to the Pasadena Art Museum and the San Francisco Museum of Art. Exhibition comprises 44 paintings, selected by Olitski from works completed within the previous four years. The greatest concentration is on spray paintings made since the spring of 1965, which are shown in relation to his earlier works.

The exhibition is discussed by Kermit Champa (*Art News*, May 1967): "Seeing Olitski's work of 1963–1967 together in a single exhibition, one is more aware of a continuity than of a planned or plotted development. At every point and in every picture the impact is that of pure, uninhibited color sensation. This sensation is . . . the very thing which Olitski has managed in various ways to control so that it becomes the means of expressing distinctly personal sensibilities. In the final analysis, what one has is 'Olitski color' rather than just color. He has possessed it and marked it out as his own."

Moves to 323 West 21st Street, New York, in June, where he sets up a studio. At the age of 45, Olitski is for the first time in a position to paint full time.

In Bennington during the summer he does a sculpture (*Bunga 45*) consisting of ten-foot-high aluminum tubes of various diameters placed upright, riveted together, and spray painted.

1968 Begins to add gel to Aqua-tec, giving greater viscosity to the paint and a tougher, more tactile quality to the surface.

Uses mops and rollers in addition to spray gun. Paints 29 works in this manner, called "Esperanza" or "Hope" series. Mixes various elements, such as varnish and pearlescent powder, with pigments.

High A Yellow is acquired by the Friends of the Whitney Museum of American Art.

One-artist exhibition, "Jules Olitski: Recent Paintings" (Feb. 21–Mar. 26), is organized by the Institute of Contemporary Art, University of Pennsylvania, in collaboration with the Hayden Gallery, Massachusetts Institute of Technology. Rosalind Krauss, in her introduction to the catalogue, has insightful things to say about space in Olitski's pictures. National Gallery of Canada buys *DD* from show at David Mirvish Gallery, Toronto (Apr. 15–May 16).

223. Olitski with Clement Greenberg. 1975

Visits England from July to September. A conversation with Anthony Caro in London prompts Olitski to make a series of twenty steel sculptures. Works in Saint Neots, near Cambridge, where a large factory is available to him. Orders tubes, domes, and sheets of aluminum pretreated with anodized colors. He cuts, shapes, and juxtaposes the aluminum pieces in an additive process to create sculptures. Sprays them with air-drying lacquer. This series is completed within a period of seven weeks.

Back in the United States, Olitski does more drawings for sculptures based on a spiral staircase and a children's slide he had seen in a New York playground. Does another sculpture, *Ohel of Volya*, related to the Saint Neots group, but spiral in form.

Shake Out is purchased by The Museum of Modern Art, New York, on December 10. This picture is later exchanged for *Willemite's Vision*.

1969 Lawrence Rubin opens a gallery on 57th Street, New York and invites Olitski to participate in the first group show in February. Others included are Caro, Noland, Louis, Stella, Arman, and Sandler.

Dayton Art Institute purchases *Intimacy* in April.

First living American artist to be given a one-artist exhibition at the Metropolitan Museum of Art, New York, entitled "The Sculpture of Jules Olitski" (Apr. 1–May 18). Henry Geldzahler selects some of the large constructions from the works executed at Saint Neots: *Whip-out, Heartbreak of Ronald and William, Six-banger, Wheels-up,* and *Whipsaw,* as well as Olitski's most recent piece, *Ohel of Volya.* Kenworth Moffett (*The Metropolitan Museum of Art Bulletin*, Apr. 1969) writes: "Jules Olitski's first major venture into sculpture is an important event, and not simply because one of America's leading painters has turned to three dimensions. The startling originality of the works and their sheer size show that he has approached his new medium with daring; he has raised issues and opened possibilities hitherto unperceived."

Joseph Hirshhorn acquires the sculpture *Whip-out,* and later, in 1974, gives it to the Hirshhorn Museum and Sculpture Garden, Washington, D. C.

Makes two small studies for sculptures in clay on plasterboard. These are the prototypes for the "ring series" of sculptures.

One-artist exhibition at Lawrence Rubin Gallery, New York (Nov. 1–Dec. 2), comprises eight paintings executed in acrylic emulsion on canvas. Subsequent exhibitions at Rubin in 1971, 1972, 1973.

1970 In the spring and summer, makes a series of small sculptures related to the disklike parts of *Ohel of Volya;* for example, *Irkutsk.* These are made of boiler (tank) ends of mild steel. Works on ring series of sculptures, returning to the theme for the next three summers. All are made in Bennington, of mild steel, lacquered to protect them from rusting.

Dayton Art Institute purchases *Zuloo.*

Albright-Knox Art Gallery, Buffalo, purchases *Second Tremor.*

1971 Moves to a larger studio at 827 Broadway, New York, in the spring. Retains 21st Street studio until the following January.

1972 Begins to use smaller and vertical format. Roughens canvas with gel, causing thickened pigment to appear more as a skin on the surface of the canvas. Uses roller or squeegee to scrape gel-thickened paint across the surface, so that variations in opacity and transparency result. Sometimes sprays color on top of this surface or brushes the edges. Colors are grayed or monotone.

Works in Bennington during the summer. Completes five sculptures from the ring series, on which he has been working intermittently during the year.

The Art Institute of Chicago purchases spray painting, *Green Marfak.*

Ken Carpenter (*Art International*, Dec. 1972) states: "The paintings of Jules Olitski seem increasingly remarkable for their tendency to elude the grasp of their audience. In part this elusiveness is due to their high quality. The best of them offer a sense of discovery that continues to emerge into consciousness long after lesser works have been fully assimilated. But even more to the point, Olitski's structure is so genuinely new that it has continually resisted perception."

1973 Begins to use Cor-ten steel in last of the ring series. The Museum of Modern Art, New York, acquires *Willemites Vision* in exchange for *Shake Out.*

Full retrospective (over 60 paintings) of Olit-

224. Olitski using slips on clay slabs at Syracuse University. June 1975

ski's paintings is organized by Kenworth Moffett, Curator of Contemporary Art, Museum of Fine Arts, Boston (Apr. 6–May 13). The exhibition travels to three other institutions: the Albright-Knox Art Gallery, Buffalo, New York; the Whitney Museum of American Art, New York; and the Pasadena Art Museum, Pasadena, California. In general, Olitski is received as a master by the local press in these cities, but dismissed by the New York art world, for example, the New York-based *Time* magazine (Robert Hughes), *Newsweek* (Douglas Davis), and *The New Yorker* (Harold Rosenberg). *The New York Times* art critic, Hilton Kramer, finds Olitski's spray paintings "vacuous" and "boring,"

"superficial" and "pretty." Further, Kramer writes: "Beyond the prettiness of the color, one feels only the cold decisions and the mechanical calculations of an artist working to fulfill a narrow historical formula." Thomas Hess, writing in *New York* magazine, is the only critic to show any appreciation of Olitski's importance, but even he is little more than respectful and very guarded. The critical recognition that Olitski has begun to receive in the mid-to-late 1960s has reached a grinding halt. From the time of this retrospective to the present, Olitski is considered *passé*, at least in New York.

Paradoxically, though, the exhibition also occurs at a high tide of Olitski's influence and ascendance to preeminence *within* the avant-garde. Larry Poons, the best of the younger painters, is quick to acknowledge his debt to Olitski (see Moffett's catalogue, p. 7). Walter Darby Bannard wrote earlier that Olitski "has preempted serious new painting. He is . . . our best painter." ("Quality, Style and Olitski," *Artforum*, Oct. 1972, p. 67). Moffett, in the catalogue to the retrospective, writes: "Olitski is at least for the moment saving painting itself as a viable modernist idiom." (ibid., p. 23.).

Purchases a home on an island on Lake Winnipesaukee, New Hampshire, where he lives from late spring to late fall.

One-man exhibition at Galerie dell'Ariete, Milan, Italy, in June and at the new André Emmerich Gallery, Zurich, Switzerland, in Jan. and July. Subsequent exhibitions at Emmerich, Zurich, in 1977, 1979.

Exhibits sculptures from ring series at Knoedler Contemporary Art, New York (Dec.).

These ring pieces are unpainted mild steel and Cor-ten steel. The new work provokes little critical interest. Subsequent exhibitions at Knoedler in 1974, 1975, 1976, 1977, 1979, 1981. Divorces second wife.

1974 Begins work in the spring on *Greenberg Variations*, the first of the new "stacked" sculpture series which will occupy him over the next several years.

Starts building a studio near his home in New Hampshire in the summer.

Charles Millard, chief curator of the Hirshhorn Museum and Sculpture Garden, writes an important article on Olitski for the *Hudson Review* (autumn 1974). Like Greenberg, Moffett, and Bannard, Millard affirms Olitski's preeminent position in modernist painting.

1975 One-artist exhibition at Waddington Gallery, London, held in conjunction with John Kasmin Ltd. (June).

Olitski continues to remain a red flag for well-known art world critics. Paul Overy, writes in *The London Times* (June 9, 1975): "Jules Olitzki's [sic] painting has always been too sweet and syrupy for me, lacking not only structure but any interest as color on canvas. In his new exhibition at Waddington II, the syrup has congealed into a glutinous scum on the surface of the paintings, yet has nothing of the relative toughness of say Tàpies 'matter paintings' of the fifties."

William S. Rubin gives the sculpture *Wheels-up* (1968) to the Whitney Museum of American Art.

1976 Participates in "New Works in Clay," Everson Museum of Art, Syracuse, New York

225. Olitski speaking at Harvard University. 1977

(Jan. 24–Apr. 4). This project is organized by Marjorie Hughto, who invites a number of avant-garde artists to Syracuse to make works in clay, a medium new to many of them. Among those participating are Helen Frankenthaler, Stanley Boxer, Michael Steiner, Anthony Caro, Larry Poons, and Friedel Dzubas, as well as Olitski. The works resulting from their visits are then exhibited in the show. Olitski is very involved in the project and exhibits fourteen works.

Exhibition of life drawings at the Noah Goldowsky Gallery, New York (May 4–June 5).

One-artist exhibition at Galerie Ulysses, Vienna, Austria (summer).

One-artist exhibition at Watson/de Nagy & Co., Houston, Texas (Sept. 11–Oct. 6).

1977 "Jules Olitski: New Sculpture" is organized by Kenworth Moffett at the Museum of Fine Arts, Boston (Apr. 26–July 3). Despite the fact that this exhibition of Olitski's "stacked"

sculptures also travels to the Hirshhorn Museum and Sculpture Garden in Washington, D.C. (July 20–Oct. 2), the show and the sculptures are ignored by the New York art world establishment and receive only local notice. Moffett, writing in the catalogue, once again makes claims for Olitski that are generally considered extravagant. Olitski's new sculpture, together with the work of Michael Steiner, is presented by Moffett as the best and most original American sculpture. While dismissing or ignoring this claim, local critics in Boston and Washington still treat the sculpture with respect, if not understanding. Thanks to Charles Millard, chief curator at the Hirshhorn Museum, that museum purchases one of the sculptures from the exhibition, *Greenberg Variations*.

As for his painting, collectors are increasingly interested, and sales are good, although Olitski is still unable to attain the prices reached by other serious abstract painters of his generation, such as Kenneth Noland, not to speak of such Pop abstractionists as Frank Stella and Ellsworth Kelly. The art world tends to regard him as too old-fashioned, too tasteful, too sensual, and, paradoxically, too sectarian, too intellectual or theoretical. Often he is left out of the annual review shows in the major museums, especially in New York. Critically, he is "out," but many young abstract painters and a small group of critics and curators continue to see him as the leading artist of our time.

Museum of Fine Arts, Boston, acquires *Tin Lizzy Green* (1964) in September.

One-artist exhibition at Amerika Haus, Berlin (Dec. 14, 1977–Jan. 6, 1978).

1978 The only break in the front of art world

226. Olitski with Kristina Gorby in his New York studio. Spring 1978

resistance is an article reviewing the Knoedler show of this year by the poet John Ashbery in *New York* magazine. Ashbery becomes the first writer not associated with the "Greenberg school" to acknowledge Olitski as a great American master (Apr. 10, pp. 69–71).

Also in April, Olitski acquires a home in the Florida Keys where he spends the winter months. His painting is done primarily in his studio in New Hampshire, although he does some painting in his New York studio as well.

Publishes the first chapter of a short story in *Partisan Review* (vol. XLV, no. 2, 1978, pp. 232–47). Olitski has been working on a long, humorous novel about an artist on and off for ten years.

Works on a sculptural commission for Gallaudet College, Washington, D.C. Also begins a sculptural dance floor, plans for which were commissioned by Harvard University and the Northeastern Pooled Common Fund.

1979 Exhibition at Knoedler Contemporary Art, New York (Apr. 21–May 10). This is a very large show for the gallery, and one of Olitski's best, but it is virtually ignored by the art press.

An important exhibition is organized by Terry Fenton, director of the Edmonton Art Gallery in Edmonton, Alberta, Canada (Sept. 12–Oct. 28). In conjunction with the show, Fenton publishes a short but ambitious text, "Jules Olitski and the Tradition of Oil Painting." The exhibition stresses Olitski's work of the 1970s, and in his essay Fenton puts the work in the context of Western oil painting. He concludes, "The past can't be duplicated. If it establishes a standard, that standard must be matched in the present. By not submitting easily to those terms, Olitski has altered them, I'm convinced, more than any artist of the past decade. In the process, he's made some of the great paintings of this century."

1980 Marries Kristina Fourgis Gorby on February 29.

One-man shows at the André Emmerich Gallery, New York (Apr 26–May 14).; the Galerie Daniel Templon, Paris, France (Oct. 25–Nov. 27), and Gallery One, Toronto, Ontario (Nov. 11–Dec. 4).

1981 One-man show at Knoedler Contemporary Art, New York (Jan. 24–Feb. 12). Participates in group show at CAPC, Bordeaux, France (Jan. 23–Mar. 21) and "International Florida Artists" at the Ringling Museum, Sarasota, Florida (Feb. 26–Apr. 26).

227. Left to right: Dr. Phyllis Meshover-Steiner, Michael Steiner, Paula de Luccia, Larry Poons, Jules Olitski, Kristina Olitski, Ted D' Esposito. Florida, 1980

STATEMENTS AND INTERVIEWS

228. *Self-Portrait, October 1974*. 1974.
Pen and pencil on paper,
14 3/8 × 9 3/8″. Private collection

1. Olitski wrote the following statement in 1966 at the time of his showing at the 33rd Venice Biennale of that year. It was slightly revised for republication in Artforum, *Jan. 1967, p. 20.*

Painting is made from inside out. I think of painting as possessed by a structure—i.e., shape and size, support and edge—but a structure born of the flow of color feeling. Color *in* color is felt at any and every place of the pictorial organization; in its immediacy—its particularity. Color must be felt throughout.

What is of importance in painting is paint. Paint can be color. Paint becomes painting when color establishes surface. The aim of paint surface (as with everything in visual art) is appearance—color that *appears* integral to material surface. Color is of inherent significance in painting. (This cannot be claimed, however, for any particular type of paint, or application of paint.)

I begin with color. The development of a color structure ultimately determines its expansion or compression—its outer edge. Outer edge is inescapable. I recognize the line it declares, as drawing. This line delineates and separates the painting from the space around and *appears to be on* the wall (strictly speaking, it remains in front of the wall). Outer edge cannot be visualized as being in some way within—it is the outermost extension of the color structure. The decision as to *where* the outer edge is, is final, not initial.

Wherever edge exists—both within a painting and at its limits—it must be felt as a necessary outcome of the color structure. Paint can be color *and* drawing when the edge of the painting is established as the final realization of the color structure.

The focus in recent painting has been on the lateral—a flat and frontal view of the surface. This has tended toward the use of flat color areas bounded by and tied inevitably to a structure composed of edges. Edge is drawing and drawing is *on* the surface. (Hard-edge or precision made line is no less drawing than any other kind.) Because the paint fills in the spaces between the edges, the color areas take on the appearance of overlay. Painting becomes subservient to drawing. When the conception of internal form is governed by edge, color (even when stained into raw canvas) appears to remain on or above the surface. I think, on the contrary, of color as being seen in and throughout, not solely on the surface.

2. The following statement was written in 1969 at the time of Olitski's sculpture show at the Metropolitan Museum of Art. It also appeared in Artforum, *Apr. 1969, p. 58.*

On Sculpture

Sculptural shape, conceived of as extensions and as further levels of the ground support, becomes, wherever placed, inseparable from the latter. It is the sense of shape not as separate object placed closely in relation to the ground, but as being in itself *derived* from the ground. *Sculptural shape is to the ground support what pictorial shape is to the painting support.*

Since edge cannot be separated from shape, drawing is everywhere to be found in sculpture. Sculpture conceived of in terms of drawing, by relying on line for direction and extension, may articulate the ground it rests on, but it does not possess the ground or the surrounding space. That sculpture is horizontal, diagonal, or vertical, that it tilts, crawls, or rises like a totem, is irrelevant. Nor does removing the pedestal suffice of itself to make sculpture possess the ground. Sculpture ought to be conceived, in its entirety, as *coming from* and *out of* and *going into* the ground. Even an overhang or "ceiling" shape is to be realized as projected ground.

Sculpture is surface in space-possessing ground. Surface is inevitably color—if only the color of the untreated surface. Sculpture *is* colored surface. Nonetheless, to be meaningful as colored surface, the work must—from beginning to end—be achieved in terms of sculptural shape. Colored surface and sculptural shape move together in space. Unlike painting, sculpture need not be available in one glance, need not be read in its entirety from any one point of view. The excitement and problem in a sculpture lies in the multiple points of view that can be seen only one at a time. Wherever you stand and look there is a single visual experience —as in painting—except that with sculpture the cumulative experience consists in looking by going *around* and *around* colored surface, while in painting it lies in looking *across* and *across* colored surface.

3. Olitski was interviewed by Friedrich Bach on June 12, 1974, and February 21, 1975, and the edited transcript appeared in Kunstwerk, *May 1975, pp. 14–24. It was republished in English in the catalogue of Olitski's sculpture show at the Boston Museum of Fine Arts in 1977.*

BACH: It was after your first sculpture, *Bunga* (1967), a sculpture of paint-sprayed aluminum tubing of various heights and diameters, bolted together, that you started to work on a whole series of painted sculpture in the fall of 1968. You are one of those well-known contemporary American painters who, in the last several years, have turned also to sculpture. What artistic problems would you say involved you in the making of sculpture?

OLITSKI: The difficulty I have in answering your question is that as an artist, one does certain things and then in retrospect makes the theory to explain to oneself what has been done. The theory I made, which I think makes some sense, is involved with notions like these. In painting, for example, the surface is flat, and you take it in at one glance. You can always see more, but each time one glance takes the whole piece in. In sculpture you can't take the object all in at one glance because it is three-dimensional. So you have to traverse it, you have to, in a sense, walk around it to possess it. So my thought was that since anything has a color— raw metal has a color—and since the shape in sculpture changes as you move around it, then the color also could change, perhaps should change, as you move around it. So I tried to make the color integral or wedded to the surface—the color changes and shape changes become one indissoluble flow.

BACH: You once mentioned that the artist who influenced you the most was Rembrandt. Would you be able to name any sculptor who has had the same meaning for your sculpture as Rembrandt had for your painting?

OLITSKI: It is true, Rembrandt is the artist whom I feel to be my master more than anyone else. But in sculpture, the sculptors to whom I was closest, at least at the time I was making those color sculptures, were Catalan Spanish sculptors who made polychrome sculptures in the twelfth century. I found myself very startled and excited by seeing their work. To be inspired by someone else's work means, I believe, feeling liberated to do one's own work.

BACH: What would you say was the greatest stimulus for you in Caro's work, and where do you feel the initial differences lay?

OLITSKI: I don't know how to answer that [laughing]. The only thing that strikes me, in terms of a response, is that Caro is a great sculptor, posing a challenge to go up against. It is the same way in painting. Noland was a great challenge for me: my response was to go up against that challenge, to go up against that vision, someone else's vision, to replace it with my own vision, to stamp it out. Not that this is done altogether consciously or deliberately— but, rather, one feels the impelling necessity for one's own vision to breathe and grow and have its life. The world of art is the marketplace of competing visions. Every work of art is an attempt on the part of its maker to impose his vision so that people see in another way. I think that the history of art is, among other things, a history of visual warfare and that a lot of creative energy comes out of that warfare.

BACH: The tension between color field and marginal drawing is a distinguishing feature of your painting since about 1964. It is also a constructive element in some of the earlier painted sculptures.

OLITSKI: Well, in sculpture I felt, and feel,

that wherever there is edge, that's an appropriate place for drawing. In painting I feel it is appropriate to draw along the outer edge or in some relation to that outer edge, because the painting itself is bounded on the outer edge where the frame is and where the end of the painting is. I wanted a kind of painting which was dominated by color and not by drawing. Whereas in sculpture it is all edge, wherever you look.

BACH: In the ring pieces the drawing element now present in the actual shaping of the forms, as edges of planes, seems to have evolved even further.

OLITSKI: Yes, I emphasized the drawing element when I made the ring pieces. The edges, the top edges of the rings and the bottom edges, I wanted to do something with those, to draw freely along the top edge and the bottom edge, to cut away and to relate all the edges together, of the inner parts to the outer parts.

BACH: Do you think that there is a connection between the curved drawing elements in some of your recent paintings—I am thinking, for instance, of *Eminent Domain-3*—and the stage you have arrived at with the drawing element in your sculpture?

OLITSKI: Yes, you may well be right. I noticed this in doing the piece, and I agree. But it is not conscious. At the time, you are so intensely involved with what you are doing, I think, that although intelligence is operating, it is hard to give a rational reason afterwards for why you did something. It just seemed right—there is a feeling of being impelled to do something.

BACH: May I ask you something about the sculpture-ground and the sculpture-nature relationship? Already your earlier sculpture reminds one to some extent of landscape forms. Now the ring pieces seem to reveal an increased groundedness of the sculpture.

OLITSKI: In a way the sculptures came out of that notion of difference—the earlier ones are trying to establish other levels of ground relative to the existing ground levels. The more recent ring pieces are more simply *plopped* down onto a ground. When I was just about to make those earlier sculptures, later shown in the Metropolitan Museum, I was visiting Avignon. The Palace of the Popes was closed that day, and I could not get inside. So I had this marvelous experience in walking around the gardens and the steps of the palace. You did not know where the level ground was, you never knew—at one point low, at another point high. You never knew quite where you were, everything being relative to everything else, so that there is no norm, so to speak, no floor. I wanted to try to get something related to that feeling—of the sculptures related to ground and coming out of the ground—of never quite knowing where one is in relation to either one.

BACH: Your earlier sculptures were painted, your sculptural work afterwards is unpainted.

OLITSKI: When I made the painted sculptures, color was playing a part in the conception of the sculpture, although the first thing I tried to make was a sculpture that worked to begin with, without added color. I felt it had to work first as sculpture, as a three-dimensional form, and it was only after I could feel that the sculpture was essentially there as a sculpture that I began to work with color onto the sculpture. And then it became a thing of both. Whereas in the ring pieces and the cor-ten steel sculptures, there is no direct involvement with color as such. It is almost, in a sense, accepting the color of the metal, which is also a color, and which, in the case of the recent sculpture, I could still work on with color—on edges, possibly. Or I might work inside the shapes with drawing in color.

BACH: Did you try that?

OLITSKI: It is on my mind. It is a possibility.

BACH: The question of the beholder-sculpture relationship is somehow intensified in your ring pieces—shapes shallowly lying together with the ground. In looking down on them, one has the impression that their intensified groundedness coincides with an increasing sense of closedness against the beholder who is trying to get close to them, that they maintain a distance.

OLITSKI: Yes, I like that. I like that in both painting and sculpture, that a work should turn its back on the viewer. I like that quality, impassive, turning its back, that you should have to go to it, to the work, and look and look again before it reveals itself. It should not be ingratiating, it should be resistant.

BACH: Although your sculpture is the opposite of a standing, anthropomorphic form, it nevertheless seems to be human-scaled.

OLITSKI: I want human scale, but I don't think about it that much. Certainly, when I am working, all I think about is the work itself, trying to realize it.

BACH: About scale, how does it work for you when you are making a sculpture?

OLITSKI: It varies in the making of the sculpture. I may conceive a sculpture that is quite large and then while working on it make it smaller, or I make a small one larger. So all that comes out in the making of the piece itself. I don't like any situation in which I am imprisoned. I like free situations—to be able to change to the very end.

BACH: Your description of how you deal with scale in sculpture seems to relate to your handling of the issue of shape in painting, when you finally cut out a painting from the expanse of canvas on the floor.

OLITSKI: Yes, for me the final decision in making a work is in responding to a question, my question: Where is it? What is its shape? I try to do that in sculpture as well. If you begin with the decision, there it is and you are imprisoned with it, limited to where the painting or sculpture is. I think making art should be a free situation—free in the sense of a highly disciplined activity—right up to the very end of making it. I want to find out where it is after I have made it. I find that exciting, to find out where it is.

BACH: What do you think is the relation between your painting and your sculptural work?

OLITSKI: I don't know. I think the problems are not the same. There are areas, of course, where they overlap.

BACH: Such as?

OLITSKI: Well, the problem of shape, of dimensions, for example, in both painting and sculpture. What is the final shape? Where does it end? Where are the edges? What is their relationship to the rest of the painting or sculpture? These are problems in both painting and sculpture. So there are, I think, areas where they intersect. But they are essentially separate languages, separate communications.

BACH: I must admit that in looking at your paintings I was sometimes distracted by the rhythmizing, dramaticizing effect of the shiny reflections of the spotlight on the gold frame.

OLITSKI: I don't think it is that crucial. But the gold stripping is, I can see, something of a distraction. I am thinking now about changing the kind of framing that I have used and will take just a wooden stripping without the gold.

BACH: You have some paintings by Hans Hofmann here in your studio.

OLITSKI: I think he is one of the greatest artists of our time. I regard him on the level of Pollock, Still—Rothko, certainly.

BACH: Do you feel a familiarity with Rothko?

OLITSKI: Not particularly. I feel more so with Hofmann. His freedom, his toughness. I don't mean to put myself in the same place with him, but I admire his powerful intelligence about painting and most of all his inspired freedom. And I want to add that I think it is a scandal that this major artist, who is a native son of Germany, has not received his due recognition in Germany. I think in America also he has still not been given his due.

BACH: Looking around in your studio, I saw a book about the Italian Primitive painters, and I had the idea that they might be of some interest for you.

OLITSKI: I like to look at their work. I remember for instance, the impression that a beautiful painting by Piero della Francesca made on me in a chapel in a little town called Monterchi. The flatness of Piero della Francesca is certainly no less than the flatness of synthetic cubism or Mondrian. In any case, flatness is arrived at through relationships. If everything in the universe were green, let us say, we would not see the color green. We can see green because there is red and yellow, etc.

BACH: On your desk across from the wall where a painting of yours is in progress, I noticed a large reproduction of Rembrandt's *Hendrickje Bathing in a Stream*, and I had the feeling of a connection.

OLITSKI: I hope you are right [laughing]! It is just extraordinary, an extraordinary painting. You can't translate its qualities into a work consciously, but it has a lot of chiaroscuro in it. And maybe that's where I am going now. I would like to bring chiaroscuro back into my painting.

BACH: When did you start with this new kind of chiaroscuro?

OLITSKI: I think since this winter or last fall. But the recent paintings relate in some ways to my work of the late fifties, the "matter" or "impasto" paintings.

BACH: Do you have a feeling why you respond to chiaroscuro in this way?

OLITSKI: No idea. But it seems to me to open something up, to get rid of "overall" painting or to destroy what some critics, referring to me now, call "empty center painting."

BACH: Your recent sculptures seem to differ from the ring pieces mainly in their opening up and becoming higher, in their being built up out of curved metal sheets of different diameters. Do you remember any motivations that brought you from the extremely ground-oriented ring pieces to this kind of building up in, for instance, the *Greenberg Variations*?

OLITSKI: What happened was that the ring pieces developed into sculptures like *Ariadne* or *King Kong*, which were already getting higher. And then Clement Greenberg happened to see a number of parts of two sculptures that were to be assembled in the field nearby. He saw them as possibilities for finished sculptures just as they were. He pointed that out to me, and it looked very interesting. From my own point of view, the pile of parts formed the essential nucleus of a sculpture that could be further developed. I developed this particular sculpture in that I took most of those parts—to begin with—and placed them as they were, with some minor changes, on top of a number of rings. So the *Greenberg Variations* started out when I took some of the parts that were to be assembled into other sculptures and placed them on top of the rings, and then further developed the sculpture by placing some enormously large remaining parts on *top* of what had become the middle section.

BACH: It seems that, whereas the "ring pieces" were more closed in on themselves, your recent work is more open, more accessible and approachable in terms of form and of size as well.

OLITSKI: Yes, they certainly are more open. There are more levels, for instance, in the *Greenberg Variations*. So that I think it would seem as if the sculpture could continue in any direction. It could go up higher to another level, or out to the sides, or wherever.

BACH: Speaking of the *Greenberg Variations*, you mentioned that it could have an additional level, thereby implying a certain openness for change in the sculpture. On the other hand, you stressed the process of finding the final form.

OLITSKI: Yes, that is true. The sculpture implies a possibility that it could go on this way or that way, up to the sides or wherever. And I like that kind of situation. Certainly, in the making of the work. But the final work should have a sense of completeness, of finality, of that

it could not be altered. Of course, this is nonsense. Vermeer, let us say, could take one of his masterpieces and alter it, and it might even be better or no worse. Or Mondrian could take one of his utterly final-looking, seemingly absolute works and change it. But as it is, it should *look* as if it cannot be altered, it should have the look of finality. I think even in the ring pieces there was the sense—for me, while making them—that there could be more rings or fewer rings, that the proportions or the relations of one to the other could be changed. The sense that you are getting with the ring pieces—that they are less open—is that they are more a matter of fewer possible relationships. The more recent sculptures, I think, are more complex in that there are more relationships, and so there are more possibilities involved of where they could go.

BACH: Have you done any clay models for new sculptures as you did for the ring pieces?

OLITSKI: No. I have some things I have not yet made. They are based on drawings and photographs, kind of photo-collages.

BACH: Do you prefer your sculpture outside?

OLITSKI: No, I prefer it indoors, but I really have no firm position. It's a relative matter. It depends on where in nature a sculpture is placed. I think you can control the space relationships better indoors. I think sculpture exists more in itself indoors, for that reason. Nature is one thing and art is something else. So I think art has more a chance of being itself in a room rather than in relation to nature.

BACH: Do you feel that recently there has been more changing and experimenting in your sculpture than in your painting?

OLITSKI: No, I feel the same way about both.

4. Speech delivered by Olitski at the University of South Carolina, Columbia, March 27, 1975.

The great French painter Henri Matisse once wrote, "He who wants to dedicate himself to painting should start by cutting off his tongue." He told his students, "You must begin by cutting off your tongue, for, starting today, you should express yourself only through plastic means. You must be what you are and cultivate this. Don't wait for inspiration. It comes while one is working."

Fortunately for us, Matisse, rare among artists for his lucid intelligence, did not follow his own advice. He wrote about art, he spoke, he gave interviews. Nonetheless Matisse is right. The language of the painter has to do with paint, not words. However, the painter being human like the rest of us, which means among other things, being vain and weak and self-indulgent, the painter all too often accepts the invitation to speak . . . and speaks and speaks.

Invariably he speaks about himself, his art, his personality, his psyche—the unique phenomenon that is himself—God's gift to the rest of us. And the rest of us . . . we listen. Why do we listen? Because we think we are going to get the *truth*, the essential meaning of art, and *that* straight from the horse's mouth. After all, who can tell us more about the meaning of the work than the creator of that work?

I suggest that it ain't necessarily so. The artist who conceived and created the work, be it a poem, a painting, a sculpture, may well be the last person in the world to explain the meaning of that work. And why should it not be so? After all, the artist's function, his reason for being, lies solely in the making of the work, the inventing of the work. The painter strives to make visually real by what he does with the materials available to him—basically paint and canvas—the vision he has of what painting is, or must be. Every decision the painter makes must be in accord with the attempt to realize that vision. I mean this in even the most prosaic sense: the choice of kinds of paint, colors, medium, brushes, canvas, or possibly paint rollers, mops, sponges or whatever, the selection of materials and what is done with them, are all in the service of the artist's vision, dictated by that vision. Necessity is indeed the mother of invention. If Rembrandt could have got the look he wanted for his paintings more effectively by using a mop, rather than a sable brush, he would have used a mop. The great Spanish painter Goya did. And if Jackson Pollock could have better achieved his vision by using a fine sable brush rather than pouring paint out of a pail onto his canvas, undoubtedly he would have done so. The artist's task is to realize his vision, not to explain it. And it's so in other fields as well.

The greatest of generals is not necessarily the best person to explain the meaning and significance of war. Tolstoy, who wasn't even there, tells it countless times better in *War and Peace* than Napoleon, who commanded the invasion of Russia, could ever have. But even the great Tolstoy is not quite so great when he tries to write about the meaning of art and literature. He *is* great when he does the one thing that he truly knows how to do, which is to write a masterpiece like *War and Peace*.

Plato said, "The poet does not know what he is saying." I take it that Plato means two things: 1. That the poet in the throes of inspiration is in the possession of, is literally being possessed by his muse . . . and 2. Implies that it is secondary and perhaps irrelevant and not his function to understand the meaning of what he has said. The sole responsibility of the poet, of the painter, is to be open and accessible to his inspirations. And that is one good reason for working a lot, so that if you are lucky enough to get inspired, it is likely you will be working at the time. Once again Matisse is correct when he says that inspiration comes, if it comes at all, usually *after* the work is begun.

There is a remark attributed to G. B. Shaw that making art requires ninety-nine percent perspiration and one percent inspiration. But that one percent is crucial. Without it, you're dead. But talking about inspiration leads to a blind alley. What is it? How is it brought about? No one quite knows. Yet many of us have experienced it. We know what it feels like. We know, even more, the effects of it, but when we try to really get hold of it, the mechanism of inspiration, the what makes it tick, we're as much at a loss as if we were trying to describe the taste of roast beef. All we can say about roast beef is it's not like Swiss cheese or clam chowder, or salami. But we can't say what it is like. It is itself . . . roast beef.

Surely inspiration is allied with imagination, fantasy and play. All these elements and more are essential to producing high art; nonetheless, the graveyards are densely packed with failed artists, artists of obvious talent, who felt themselves inspired and who did not entirely lack creative imagination, or the capacity for play. Alas, one must have, in addition to the rest, something to say, and the passionate curiosity and courage, to enable oneself to undertake the voyage of discovery, to find what one has to say and how to say it. This, I think, is where the real excitement of making art lies.

The bare canvas, as for the poet or composer, the unmarked page, presents a chaos of possibilities. A chaos of speculative projected possibilities. Chaos is not to be confused with freedom. "Anything goes" is not what making art is about. The serious artist chooses, selects, shapes and discards what is not essential to his purpose. He or she is ruthlessly willful in the quest to achieve the desired end, an ordered, coherent, expressive work of art, expressive in the case of painting of what the painter's vision of painting is. And that vision, if it is authentic, sooner or later *imposes* itself upon the rest of us. As Igor Stravinsky wrote in his book, *Poetics of Music*, "The artist imposes a culture upon himself and ends by imposing it upon others. That is how tradition becomes established."

I believe we see and hear and feel and experience our reality differently than we would have without the creative visions imposed upon us by the great visionaries of art, and here I must include, of science as well, indeed any area of intellectual and creative work that has an effect on our sense of reality. I emphasize the word *imposed*. In fact I would go on to say that the history of art and science, in a sense, can be seen as a history of warfare, of competing visions, endlessly embattled and challenging one another, one after the other overtaking and over-running the other, imposing new visions of art and reality upon human consciousness. Now, I do not mean that one displaces or destroys the other. Einstein, Oppenheimer, do not wipe out Isaac Newton or Galileo. Dewey and Heidegger do not wipe out Plato and Aristotle. Pollock does not wipe out Rembrandt. It is simply that one grows out of the others and especially out of its challenge to the others. That is what tradition is about. Our art one hopes will be the traditional art of another time. Other visions will arise and overcome ours.

And incidentally, do you think if the great Rembrandt, whom I happen to regard as my master, was painting today, do you think he would be painting Rembrandts? Assuredly he would be painting pictures that would be in accord with his creative vision of the reality of now. There is of course, no way of knowing what his paintings would be like if he were painting today, but I would bet my last dollar that his art would be challenging the conventions of the art of our time, just as he did in his own time, and this is what every major artist, in the modern age, at least since the Renaissance, has done in his time. And this goes as much for Ingres and Poussin and Manet in their times as for Pollock and Hofmann and Noland and Caro in our time.

Finally I would say there is nothing more useful for the serious artist than resistance, the brick wall, something worthwhile to go up against, to be challenged by. This is precisely the situation in which inspiration and creative imagination are unlocked and unleashed. "Challenge the influential master," Cézanne said. The artists must present us with the vision of what art is to look like, how we are to see and feel and experience our reality. And what a blessing that challenge is for all those who do creative work. As Marcel Proust put it, "A powerful idea can communicate some of its strength to him who challenges it."

So I think curiosity, the urge to discover, the incitement of a major challenge, the will to impose one's artistic vision so that we all see and experience differently than before, all these have to do with making art. As for the meaning of art, as I said, I don't have to deal with that. I will merely quote the last line of the poem *Apollo* by Rainer Maria Rilke, where the poet has the beautiful statue of Apollo speak to the viewer. The statue says, "You must change your life."

5. An interview with Judith Dayton on October 23, 1977.

DAYTON: Was there a particular reason why you tended toward painting in the beginning?
OLITSKI: It depends upon when we are talking about, because in my mind it is hard to say that there was a specific direction like painting as opposed to sculpture or sculpture as opposed to painting. I can remembe rwanting to be a sculptor and I was, in fact, even as a student. At the National Academy of Design I started with painting and drawing, but I would go at night to the Beaux Arts Institute and study sculpture. Also, there was an art school on East Broadway, the Educational Alliance, that I would go to at night and work at sculpture, mostly in plaster of paris, clay, etc. Then, when I went to Paris on the GI Bill after the Second World War, it was to enroll at the Zadkine School of Sculpture. So, sculpture was very much in the forefront of my interest at the time.

DAYTON: Was sculpture something that you always wanted to get back to and it was just a question of being the right time, or did it not seem to be fitting in with where you were going?
OLITSKI: Probably all of those things, although how conscious any of that is, I am not sure. I seem to be someone who is very vulnerable. I don't know how to explain it, not that it's a mystery, but something will happen or someone will say something, or it will be in front of me, and I'll get very involved in that thing if I am open to it.

A lot of the sculpture in recent years developed out of a meeting in London, an invitation from Tony Caro to use his studio. I didn't use his studio, and it's fortunate for him that I didn't [laughing]. I might have messed it up. I suddenly found there were a lot of things that had evidently been going on in my mind about sculpture. If Tony hadn't made that generous offer, I would have continued going about what I was doing at the time, and whatever was going on in my mind about making sculpture may have continued going on there, without my being aware of it. It would have surfaced possibly at some other time or, perhaps, never surfaced. That makes me sound, I suppose, a bit mindless —as if things just happened to me—maybe that is true. I think I would accept that to some extent. Why not?
DAYTON: Would you say that you continually react to situations?
OLITSKI: Well, there is another thing that goes on that might be worth mentioning. I tend to react, to go up against. I find out what I think and want when I am confronted with what I'm against, and this impels some outpouring of

energy, in a creative sense, in those areas. Of course that is just one side of the coin, but I have noticed that side in myself.

DAYTON: Did sculpture, then, represent a challenge to you?

OLITSKI: Yes, I think there is something here that has to do with challenge. If you make art, you have a plastic vision of what it is that you are trying to express. I don't mean that you have a specifically laid out, clear as a map or a chart, kind of vision. It may be something that you can almost see, like Moses could see the Promised Land, but he never could get to it. I think that's the great frustration of art. You can almost see it, it's on the other side of the river, you can almost get to it. You never do quite get to it. Sometimes you get closer or less close, or sometimes in getting to it you come upon something else which leads you elsewhere, which also becomes part of what you are after.

DAYTON: You once said you would like to spray colors up into the air and have the colors somehow remain suspended there.

OLITSKI: Yes, it was said by me, as a kind of joke, but in response to and reacting against something that someone else was saying that had to do with art, in this case Tony Caro. Tony said something, I think he wanted to emphasize the materiality of sculpture, the denseness or the weight. I think that I may have responded almost facetiously (I am not sure of all this in retrospect), that I wanted an art that was the opposite to materiality. Let's say in painting, if I could just have a spray of color that somehow remained intact. Shortly thereafter, it struck me that like some funny things said, there was something being said internally within that, and, I think

almost perhaps the very next day I went out and rented a spray gun and tried to do it. This then led to a whole development for me in my work that I was very serious about. At the same time, having used a word like serious in parentheses here, it might be useful to emphasize the role of play in making art. Sure it's serious, making art, but it involves play and play is to be taken seriously . . . children do.

DAYTON: Why did you choose steel as the medium of your most recent sculptures? Their lightness seemed to contradict the heaviness of steel.

OLITSKI: The St. Neots sculptures were all made of aluminum, and why aluminum? One reason was, and this solely had to do with what I am calling the pragmatic or practical aspect, it was lighter, it was easier to move, to handle. Since I, as a painter, largely had been one who worked, and still does, by himself, I wanted a material that I could handle by myself, whereas mild steel or Cor-ten is so heavy. You can't take a piece and put it over here and another there and so on, whereas I could move around fairly big pieces of aluminum and juxtapose them and put them next to one another and work in a way that was familiar to me. I tried to set up a system, in fact, in making the St. Neots sculptures that was comparable for me to the way I paint, a system that would have in it the possibilities for freedom, for being free, that one has in painting. You know, you have all kinds of colors at hand, you can take this color or you can take that color. You can change things very quickly in painting. What I did in the St. Neots system was to order beforehand hundreds of color-anodized shapes. So I did have some notion, in those sculptures,

of color, and color related to sculpture, and this gave me, to begin with, a situation comparable to painting where I could choose this color, this shape, and then change it. There is very little of the anodized color itself remaining in those sculptures, although sometimes it is there under a glaze or color and is apparent that way. There was to some extent just a simple practical reason for choosing aluminum. It wasn't that I was so thrilled by the notion of aluminum or I am so thrilled by the notion of Cor-ten steel or mild steel. A material for me is simply something that serves a purpose, gets me where I want to be. I share very little of that mystique about material that some artists seem to have, or craftsmen in particular. I notice how potters just adore clay, or they say they love it and they love to immerse themselves in it, and I think etchers have this as well. I don't get any special thrill out of putting my hand into a pail of paint or stroking some cold Cor-ten steel. The aluminum played its role. I then went to mild steel and then to Cor-ten steel. There were those aspects, aesthetic we call them, that played a part in how something should feel and look and notions about density and weight or lightness. Yes, all these come into play. How conscious I am at the time of such things I am not at all sure. Let me put it this way. First, you make the thing, then you make the theory, and maybe it comes then only to make you feel more secure about what you have made. Maybe I am being a little too harsh here, because the theory may be quite correct. For example, I wrote a statement once about color painting. It appeared first in the Venice Biennial catalogue in 1966, I think. I afterward revised it slightly. The main notion of what I said there remained, and it had to do with drawing in relation to color and where drawing was appropriate in painting. Now, I find the paintings that I have been doing in recent years violate everything that I said about where drawing was realizable in painting. When someone recently pointed this out, I came up with the theory that explained these recent paintings, which was just as reasonable, it seemed to me, as the earlier theory which explained those earlier paintings. Now I can and do live with both of these.

DAYTON: Are there connections between the spray-gun paintings and the paintings you are currently involved with, or do you find you are taking off in a totally new direction?

OLITSKI: I think things take their course and one thing leads to another. You do something. You become aware of something because that something that you intended did not come out as you intended, or it did but something else became apparent, and the something else someone else may even point out to you. We're not always aware of what we do in painting and in art. What I am getting at, I think, is that you don't make art in a vacuum. If it has to do with communications, which I think it does, there is someone that you are communicating to.

DAYTON: Would you say that your interest in texture or your interest in other elements of painting form connections between your works?

OLITSKI: I could look at my painting and say, "Well, it has to do with texture, surface," but I would then want to go on to say that all painting has to do with texture and surface and that my painting, like anyone else's, always has had to do with texture and surface because one of the basic things in a painting is its surface. Even before anything is put onto canvas, it already

has a surface. Some critics made a point about the stained paintings some of us were doing, saying that the surface of the canvas, the thing itself, was stained with the color so that you had a kind of purity of color and material, the canvas, but for me, this was surface. So from there, I could say to myself and sometimes do, "Well, there are all kinds of surfaces that paint lends itself to, and painting, to some extent, seems to be necessarily about paint." Paint is part of it . . . well, paint and what can be exploited here. I think making art is an exploiting, among other things, of the material and resources and what you can do with them in terms of your vision of this thing. One can never quite describe what that vision is, and I think that that, incidentally, is a good thing: I am somewhat suspicious of artists who know too much about what they are doing and can talk too intelligently about what they have done.

DAYTON: I recently saw a silkscreen of yours. It seemed that in the case of the silkscreen you were exploiting the nature of the ink and the surface of the print. Does this bear any relationship to your painting?

OLITSKI: Yes, I think with the silkscreen, and again we are talking about something that was done quite a few years ago, I did want to get the feeling and look of surface. A silkscreen, of course, is a flat sheet of paper, and I didn't want a kind of poster look that a lot of silkscreens have, or a kind of mechanical look. I did want the look of surface and did explore ways with the technicians of getting that look. I sprayed to get that on the silk, so it was a conscious choice to try and get that.

DAYTON: You drew on the edges of the silkscreen and also included some rectangles at the

bottom of the print, an orange one and a white one specifically.

OLITSKI: This is an example for me of what I was saying earlier of how the theory comes afterwards. Now, at that time, in a number of paintings there were these bits, sometimes rectangles, sometimes dots of color close to the edges of the paintings or drawings that I was doing. *Tin Lizzy Green* and other paintings of the time have this as well as the silkscreens. The theory, as I may have expressed it at the time, was that this gave me a way of being free or implied a kind of freedom of introducing any number of colors into a painting, drawing, or the pastels I was doing, or the silkscreens. If I put in one or two dots of color, rectangles of color, what was also clear was that I could put in a dozen. I could put in a hundred, or limit myself, or let it expand, and these colors were also elements of drawing. Being in a sense drawing, they had to be, at least in those works at that time, close to the edge of the shape itself. For me it seemed that the shape of a canvas, whether it was shaped canvas or a rectangle, which was also a shape, or a circle, you couldn't get away from . . . the fact that it's a shape. Everything has its shape, and the painting has a delimited shape. Finally you decide that this is where the painting is and this is the shape of it. Well, the outer shape, the limit, is a line, and a line is drawing. Sculpture in that sense is all drawing. Every angle that you look at has its configuration and its outer edge; in fact, I suppose I would have to say that sculpture has more drawing in it than painting in that sense, internally as well as throughout. Any angle which you look at has it. When I am making something, I am not at all sure that I am doing anything with a specific, coherent, worked-out notion. When I put that dot of color on the side in that kind of relation to the edge, I don't think that it's because I have thought it out so coherently and precisely. The truth is probably more that, for whatever reason, I feel impelled to do that, without much, if any, conscious prethought. Conscious or unconscious, I believe intelligence is operative here. What we call inspiration involves intelligence, soul, spirit, character, all that is going on during the making of the thing. Afterwards, it's almost impossible and, perhaps, is impossible to adequately say just what happens. This applies as well (at least from the little bit of reading I have done) to scientific thinking when some major scientific breakthrough has been made. Mathematicians, physicists, and astronomers frequently afterwards describe the experience as a kind of creative experience that is familiar to artists who don't know quite what was going on in their minds. Among the things which I think are involved with intelligence and thinking are possibilities, projections, choices—holding in your mind at one and the same time any number of possibilities, in visualizing what might happen, and making these choices, so that the whole thing becomes so multilayered and so intense that afterward I certainly cannot remember.

DAYTON: Earlier you were talking about the edge of the painting being a line and how that related to your sculpture. The drawing in many of your paintings seems very spontaneous and loose in character. The lines in the ring series seem relatively controlled at first and then evolve into a looser broken arrangement in sculptures like *Hybrid T*. Does your painting affect your sculpture and vice versa as you are working?

OLITSKI: I tend to go off in two directions here. One is that the chances are that one thing affects another, consciously or unconsciously, wittingly or unwittingly. At the same time, my notion is that these are rather separate, distinct languages, that is, painting is a language. It is a different language than writing or singing or composing with notes. Now, both painting and sculpture are visual art, but they are separate languages. They have elements that are true in both. You can point to these—drawing, line—in a shape, and a painting does have a shape, as a sculpture does. So, they share certain similarities but, nonetheless, one is a painting and one is a sculpture and obviously the two are different. When I am making a sculpture, thinking about painting is of no help to me. All I am thinking about is what is appropriate to the making of a sculpture. This involves many notions, feelings, and visions of what constitutes a sculpture, and I think what could be added here that is extremely important in the making of the sculpture, as in the making of the painting, as in the writing of fiction, or whatever, is what is not appropriate and what can be left out, and done away with. Again, I think intelligence has some role here. It's when people introduce into their action what is not appropriate that they are odd or crazy. This is not essential. I don't want to make it sound like art is a matter of "good taste," not at all. I think high art is always disturbing, not necessarily at all in good taste. In fact, it rocks conventions. It goes against. High art always goes against the accepted, the conventions of the time. It is resisted because it makes us in some way uncomfort-

able. It poses other possibilities for seeing, for feeling, for experiencing.

DAYTON: How do you think your art reflects that whole idea of confronting the viewer?

OLITSKI: I don't really think that it's for me to say. Other people can and do. All I think I'll permit myself to say here is that to the extent that there continues to be some controversy about my art, that's good!

DAYTON: So, perhaps then, the whole idea of confrontation is something that comes out of of the piece. It's not something that you are thinking of beforehand.

OLITSKI: No, you're not; you don't say to yourself, and I don't think it's useful or gets you anywhere to say to yourself, "Well, I am going to be original." I think that if an artist is original, he doesn't have to decide to be. It will come out of his being. It is part of his or her entire outlook, and this is shaped by innumerable factors, most of which we are probably not even aware of.

DAYTON: I have noticed that your recent work has been compared to that of Picasso and Cubism. Do you think that this is a valid connection?

OLITSKI: What comes up in my mind is an essay by E. A Carmean about a Cubist painting by Picasso and a painting of mine, and he noticed some similarities in the two, and he made a point about it. That's the only place that I have ever noticed where some work of mine was compared to a Cubist work. I looked at the two photographs that he used for illustration of the two paintings, and I could see, certainly, some superficial resemblances, but the notions that Picasso was working with and that I was working with at the time, I don't think really related to each other. Of course, as a painter in the twentieth century, I am familiar with Cubist painting and have been influenced by it as have most other Western artists of the twentieth century. But I could say the same, and maybe with even more reality, about Titian, Rubens, and Rembrandt and any number of artists whom I have been deeply influenced by as part of my growing up.

DAYTON: You have mentioned an interest in Rembrandt before. Are there any particular ways that you feel that you have been influenced by Rembrandt or any other artist?

OLITSKI: Yes, of course, in a few specific ways. One, to begin with, as a young man seeing Rembrandts, and being knocked over by them and wanting to make paintings like them. When I began as an art student, it was with the notion of being a portrait painter and being able to make paintings that looked like Rembrandts. Well, that has changed considerably, but I still look at Rembrandt in terms of his art as a very pure visual art, because of what he did with surface and how he put a painting together; the way it flows across and possesses the canvas, coming, going, in and out, and at the same time retains its unity across the entire surface. There are no holes. Rembrandt's chiaroscuro envelops the entire surface. There is no pulling apart. Now, there is something about that notion that I respond to and that I would like to achieve in my own terms when I talk of the artist's vision. Now, this may not be apparent to anyone in my work. Nonetheless, it is there. So, I look at Rembrandt in those terms. Among the paintings that I have in my studio that are reproductions, is the *Polish Rider* of Rembrandt, and it sits there on the wall and is the kind of an ideal of pure painting I try to achieve in my own terms. Ingres

is another whom I regard as a master. Well, there are any number, Corot, Vermeer. . . . But, these things have to do with color, with surface, with form, with ways of possessing the canvas. Matisse did it in his way; Matisse is someone who can make me cry when I feel his feeling, but it is not my way. His color, and his feeling of the color, and how the expanse of it would determine its shape and where it ended and another color began. To me, that approach to color sets up a drawing structure within the painting that is not my way. This doesn't mean that it's bad because I am opposed to it, but it is not in conformity with my own feelings and notions about color, drawing, and what a painting is to look like and come out of.

DAYTON: I got the impression that you were reluctant to part with *Tin Lizzy Green* and that perhaps it was a favorite painting of yours. Is this true?

OLITSKI: Yes, it's true. I was reluctant to give it up but not for the most idealistic conceivable reason. Certainly, one reason was a practical reason. I tend to keep some number of works of my own for myself, and *Tin Lizzy Green* was from a period of my paintings of which I have very few remaining. Then, there are reasons that have to do with commerce, value, and increase of value. These things, whether we like them or not, are to be considered. Mainly, I think that *Tin Lizzy Green* was a good example of the kind of painting that I was doing in 1964, and I do have a special feeling for that painting.

DAYTON: Are there any other paintings that you feel are especially good? For what reasons do you feel that they are better than others?

OLITSKI: Again, I don't know. I was almost going to say that's something I prefer to leave

to other people to say. Part of that is because I find that after I've done a painting and it's gone from me, I tend to look at the painting as if it was done by someone else. I will look at it and maybe have a deep emotional response, but it's in the same way that I would respond to a painting by someone else. So, I don't think of it in terms of, oh yes, that's a favorite painting of mine. I come to look at it rather critically and sometimes I have had the experience of seeing a painting of mine and for a moment not recognizing it and then being pleased to find out that I had done that painting.

DAYTON: Getting back to the St. Neots sculptures, the shapes seemed to flow out, and the colors seemed to spread beyond the limits of the surface.

OLITSKI: Yes, those notions were involved and implicit in the work, and as I said earlier, theory and rationalization frequently you make up afterwards. In any case, I was involved with some notions of one color flowing into another. I think *Tin Lizzy Green* has that kind of notion in it. Although sculpture is something that you traverse in order to take in the whole thing. It's not like a painting which each instant you can take it in at one and the same time. You may see different things each time you take that look, but what you see is there in that instant. Sculpture generally cannot be taken in entirely from one instant of time and place. As you move around it, it changes. The St. Neots sculptures have that notion in them. Also, the notion of color as something that flows and changes as it flows, and of shape that changes as you traverse, can live together happily. The effect of the sculptures, at least as I read it and heard it from the viewers, was that a lot of people were rather startled by the colors and did not have a very happy experience. The color as it was being used in those sculptures was not the way we had become accustomed to the use of paint on sculpture in our time. That was the effect. What the effect of those sculptures would be if they were shown today, I don't know. I have a hunch it would be just the same feelings of anger and outrage, and disgust.

DAYTON : Do you think that the response of the people to those sculptures had any effect on your changing over to colorless sculpture ?

OLITSKI : I would like to say, "Oh, no, absolutely not, that I am myself, so courageous and indifferent to public opinion, and so on." In fact, I think I will say that, because I think it's true. The reason is that one thing leads into another and that things take their course, and that's how art gets made. Why move from aluminum to steel, from painted surface to unpainted surface ? Some of the reasons were simple, practical reasons; pragmatic reasons concerning technical problems came into play. One of the problems with the aluminum painted polychrome sculptures was my fear that because they were light in weight and had this painted surface, they would not survive weather conditions if they were outside. If I could get past some of those technical problems, I would love to make some painted sculptures again, and I am sure that I will have another crack at that. So, those were some considerations, and also the notion of simply accepting the given color of steel and what could be done with varnishes, oil, with Cor-ten steel and rust. But look, even in the polychrome sculptures, the so-called St. Neots sculptures, my primary concern was that before a sculpture would leave my hand, it had

to work as a sculpture. I still think that the role of color can be exploited in modern sculpture and my attempt was an attempt in that direction, but I can live with sculpture that I make that has no color in it, apart from the given color that I can play with of the steel itself.

DAYTON : One of the reasons that you went to sculpture was that the viewer had to move around it. It couldn't all be taken in from one point. Ken Moffett once said that the ring sculptures turned their back on the viewer. I thought that was an interesting comment.

OLITSKI : This has to do with a qualitative situation. I prefer in my own art a look that in some ways says, "I'm not asking to be liked." You have to come to it. It's hard to describe these things. In the sculpture, or those sculptures that you are talking about, I wanted a kind of plopped-down look. I liked that. It shouldn't be ingratiating. Now, some works of mine may have this look more than others, and why not ? We're not the same all of the time. Some work may be more inviting than others. I still would want my art work to have some distance between itself and the viewer. It shouldn't be too acceptable. My complaint about the so-called avant-garde art of our time, is that it is so accessible, so easy. It's so asking to be liked.

DAYTON : Your most recent sculptures, for example, those that were on exhibit at the Boston Museum of Fine Arts this past summer, seem to have less of that quality of turning their backs. There's a lot of folding in and out, they seemed very light.

OLITSKI : Again, I don't think it is for me to say. The ring sculptures came out of some things I was doing with clay that developed that way. I don't know what motivated them. The recent

sculptures were inspired from some drawings that I was making for sculpture. When I sat down and picked up the crayon and began drawing, the drawings that appeared were not what I had had in mind. They just took off in this direction and I went with it, which I tend to do in making my art. I think you just have to believe in what you are making. Some faith is involved here. Very little is known about any of this. What is inspiration, for example ? How much does it count ? We know it's there and we know that it happens. For my part, I think nothing really happens without it. If you take a very great artist, who is not inspired, it's an indifferent work that is produced. Somehow, it doesn't ring, it doesn't convince us. Inspiration is something that you can't legislate. My own experience is that it comes in the course of the work, it happens. Well, I like making art. I get some of my kicks from the experience of it, but there are certainly times when I can think of other things I would prefer to do. Sometimes I may find myself trying to make a painting or sculpture and it's not really what I wanted to be doing at the time. Nonetheless, what frequently happens is that once you begin, something takes over, and the excitement, the intensity, and the adventure of it, the joy and the terror happen, and if you're fortunate, what we call inspiration takes place. That's great when that happens, but it doesn't generally happen beforehand. It happens in the making, which is a good reason why you have to work a hell of a lot. Oblomov, the character in that nineteenth-century Russian novel, lies on his couch thinking, dreaming great inspirational visions. This doesn't produce work. One thing that occurs to me is the art exists only if there is someone to see the art. The viewer is as important as the artist. It's true that great art is a rarity; a great viewer is a rarity, too. It's not only the artist who sees the great original art. In fact, the artists are frequently the last ones to see and acknowledge the great art that is being made. Today, we read and talk about a great original artist like Jackson Pollock and the assumption is that his peers recognized his work. The truth is that most of them thought that Pollock was a kind of buffoon. This was true for Cézanne as well. Pissarro recognized Cézanne as a major artist but most didn't, and for that matter, Cézanne himself had some serious doubts about his art. There are more people painting today and there are more people looking, but a great artist is a rarity and a great see-er even more rare. Art is an accepted kind of thing today. I think most artists today traveling abroad don't hesitate to put "artist" on their passport when they are asked what their occupation is. Not so long ago, that wasn't the situation at all, certainly in America. If you happened to be a professor teaching art in a university, the chances are you would write that on your passport or on an official document, rather than "artist." There has been a big change in the situation, certainly of American art, certainly in the attitude of the public. What remains constant, though, is the rarity of people, and this includes critics, who can really see and look and experience.

DAYTON: Is it necessarily implied that a good viewer sees what the artist intended?

OLITSKI: I think a good viewer somehow goes right to what's essential in the art. I'm not sure it's even possible to say what it is explicitly. Some of what we have talked about here are things that are sensed. A whole multitude of things enter into it, like your feeling about someone you love. If you are asked to say exactly what the quality of this love is, it is very difficult. There are things that you sense and discern somehow and you don't even know quite why. Why do you like this person and not that person? Why do you love this person, this landscape, and not that? Why is there a kind of conjoining of experience of the artist and the viewer so that what is essential in that work is being experienced by both? Our experience, our intelligence tell us what and whom to love. There are so few rare human beings, and great art is rare—it's an honor. Sometimes the two meet. It's not the usual situation. It doesn't matter if people like your art or don't like it. If the work is any good, at least one person will see it.

DAYTON: After you cut a canvas, do you ever look back and wish that you had stopped sooner?

OLITSKI: I've had the experience, and I'm sure other artists have, of not stopping in time and losing something. Sometimes I've been fortunate to get something else that is better or that led to something else. I think it useful not to be precious about one's own work, to take the risk of altering or destroying. It's essential, in fact, not to be happy with my own work. I'm rarely pleased. We find Cézanne saying constantly "I hadn't *realized* my vision." I'm not sure I am quoting him exactly, but he does use the word realize—pursuing that attempt to realize. In order to do that you have to take the risk of destroying something that is good. Probably works you did in the past are best left alone. That's what you felt and had to say at that time. There is a temptation to constantly revise. You can't change the mistakes in your life very easily. In art you can. You can take this painting and destroy it, if you think it was a mistake, but with life you can't do that. It's one of the nice things about painting or making works of art— you can alter it, you can wipe it out and make it something else in a moment. In painting it is easier and quicker than in sculpture, and that's a very attractive thing, I find.

6. Olitski wrote the following statement for Partisan Review *(vol. XLII, no. 4, 1978, pp. 560–61) as part of a symposium. Various painters, sculptors, and critics were asked to contribute to a discussion on the differences between the art scene of the 1940s and '50s and that of the late '70s.*

I was not at all on the scene in the forties and barely, if at all, in the late fifties. I don't really feel on the scene today either. Concerning present taste and sensibility, I am bemused by collectors and museum people who dote equally, at one and the same time, upon their David Smith *and* their George Segal, upon their Kenneth Noland *and* their James Rosenquist, upon their Anthony Caro *and* their Alexander Calder. When did it begin? Did the few collectors twenty or thirty years ago of Pollock and Still also go for Ben Shahn and Corbino? In the later nineteenth century the collectors and critics who went for Monet and Pissarro didn't go for Bouguereau and Meissonier too. (This easy acceptance in our time of high art alongside lesser or even meretricious art was first brought to my attention by Clement Greenberg in a talk he gave at Bennington College eight or nine years ago.)

Attitude toward money? Maybe what's new is the expectation of artists that real money is to be made in the making and selling of art. Art dealers are quite properly out to make a profit. I doubt there has been any change in their area. An art market of one sort or another has existed for at least several centuries, which certainly hasn't prevented great art from being made, or great artists from practicing their art. Artists always hope that one day they will find their Kahnweiler. But the sad truth is there are no Kahnweilers. Even Kahnweiler wasn't Kahnweiler, at least not as he has been pictured in retrospect. Money in itself doesn't corrupt. One has to be accessible to corruption. Money can be a help, especially when you have a family. That ought to be obvious.

As to the kind of painting and sculpture being done, I don't think a time that has produced a Noland, a Caro, among at least an armful of both younger and older artists, has anything to be apologetic for.

I suppose one enormous difference, maybe unique to recent times, is the emergence of artists in their twenties and early thirties (there may even be some in their teens, though I don't know any), who are given major shows in respectable galleries and museums and are taken very seriously by the art public, art critics, collectors, and maybe most damagingly of all, by themselves. The young artist who feels that every move he makes is being watched by critics and collectors, by his peers and the public, not unnaturally may come to have a vested interest in maintaining his success. One painter I know—one who survived his youthful success and is now working better than ever—said to me one day, rather plaintively, "It was like growing up in public." There is value in long years of obscurity, if one doesn't go insane or become suicidal, in that, simply because nobody is looking, the habit of fooling around and trying things out gets ingrained. This seems to be true for painters and sculptors (with some exceptions) in a way that it isn't for poets, composers, mathematicians, or chess masters.

It's hard enough to take risks if you feel you have something to lose. And it's that much harder if you have something to lose at about the same time you've begun to shave. I don't think it occurred to serious young artists of my generation (I am fifty-six years old now) that money and fame would be there at the very outset of our careers. At least I myself never thought it. It simply wasn't a part of the reality of my twenties, thirties, or early forties.

There are, of course, other differences between then and now. There is an increasing emphasis on the tying of art and the marketplace to social causes, politics, certain groups or blocs of people. To my mind art is a democratic situation; anyone can look at it or make it, and everyone should have his or her chance to be seen, if the work has anything to it. That's just it. Quality must remain the paramount concern. The quality of the art and the quality of the viewer.

©1978 *Partisan Review*

7. Olitski wrote the following while he was working on a sculptural dance floor for Harvard University in 1979. The statement is scheduled to be published in Partisan Review.

The ground is essential to dance; dancers move on it, rise from it, and return to it. However, and probably since its beginnings, the relating of dance to ground has not been sufficiently exploited. My guess is that the earliest dancer, the original choreographer, took the shape of the ground into account, and seldom, if ever, chose flat ground. It is possible he (or she) chose in each instance a particular site, which because of its slope, contour, or whatever, lent itself to, even inspired, the expressive movements of the dance, just as it seems the earliest painters chose certain caves which had useful wall surfaces and made use of these surfaces so that an expressive relatedness was maintained between wall and painting.

The direction taken by dance since then (for whatever reasons of convenience and culture) has been toward a flat surface (the use of stage props and decor does not alter the fact). This need not have been so. Flatness of support may or may not be inherent in the nature of painting, but in dance, which moves from the ground, above it, and back on to it and so on—I see no compelling necessity for a *flat* support. Art which moves calls somehow for a more *involved* ground support than art which does not move.

Dance is dependent upon, obviously inconceivable without, ground support. One calls forth the other. An expressive dialogue should come into play, one that seeks climax and resolution. It is a general lack of intimate, *expres-*

sive dialogue betwixt and between floor and dance that I point to. I am reminded, and with delight, by Clement Greenberg, of that scene in an old film where Bill "Bojangles" Robinson does a dance on a staircase. Here was an example of dance and support being expressively inseparable.

It is paradoxical that dance, which has nothing to do with flatness, should seek it. Dance ought not to seek flatness, and I am not speaking now of the flatness of floor, but that of dance itself. Flatness is not of the essence of dance (as it can be maintained it is of painting); how can it be when there is *three-dimensional movement*? Nonetheless, unless I am quite mistaken, some dance, and that among the best of our time —I think of George Balanchine's choreography of Stravinsky's *Agon* and Jerome Robbins' choreography of Bach's the *Goldberg Variations* —have sought to emulate, at least qualitatively, the "flatness" of modernist painting. And they succeed, to the extent that they do succeed, because of the austere purity and formality of limited movement danced on a two-dimensional support—a kind of dance equivalent to the "stillness" of Picasso's synthetic cubism. Presumptuous as it is—and it is—I am saying dance can be more if it exploits the ground upon which it moves and *makes* the ground *more one with itself.*

Where is it written that the dance floor must be flat? *Where* the *necessity*? I suggest there are potentialities for dance stemming from the very nature of dance and only waiting to be made significant when choreographer and dancer examine the literal ground on which they stand. It ought to be apparent, for example, that if a dancer does not *always* descend to the same level from which he has ascended, that opens visual as well as movement possibilities to the way three-dimensional forms move in relation to the space and support they move in around them.

It is in *relation* to the floor as well as to space that dance arises, moves, descends, and so on. I think choreography might take this notion into account: before there can be a dance, there ought to be a floor—a floor containing more than one level—that relates to the dance. Why not have the inner reality of the dance—its syntax, so to speak—be inspired by the floor itself? Such a multi-leveled floor would be in a more immediate and involved relation to the dancer's movement in space (and the dancer to it) than the usual two-dimensional floor. What I am suggesting is that (at least for *pure* dance), first a floor be conceived and *then* the choreography envisioned in relation to that floor.

It could work the other way as well: the choreographer envisions a dance and then designs a floor unique to that dance.

All I'm suggesting is that since the floor is inseparable from the dance, more can be developed from this relationship than there has been (to my knowledge at any rate).

8. *Based upon excerpts from Olitski's talk, Sept. 22, 1979, at the Edmonton Art Gallery, Edmonton, Alberta.*

All that is required of the artist, all that ought and should be required, is the making of good art. I place no emphasis on originality.

All good art is original, beyond a certain level.*

I happen to believe that good art has to come from character. The evidence on all sides is that some art, some very great art—and I can think of some acquaintances—has been made by people you wouldn't want to have anything to do with apart from the fact that they happen to make good art. How to explain this? There are other people I know who are nice, but just don't have what's needed to make a painting or a sculpture or a poem come alive in ways that affect our experience. How to fathom this paradox, if what I believe about the role of character to be true? I don't know, and I don't know of anyone else who does.

A lot of what I've just said applies to the beholder too. You can be awful as a human being and yet have this thing of really seeing great art.

I happened to see a documentary on TV about Albert Einstein, and there he is talking about scientists and the making of science. He said: "The scientist must have a nature that is inquisitive and he must play." That's true as well for the artist and for the making of art.

The making of good art requires—beyond the other gifts of unique quality: talent, intelligence and vision—a capacity for play brought to a heightened level that I can only describe as deeply inquiring and serious play. Maybe we all begin, in some degree, with those qualities and capacities, but in short order they are knocked out of our heads and hearts.

---

* Said to me in conversation by Clement Greenberg.

When you see your own originality, it frightens you. The temptation is to return the work to the familiar.*

Maybe just here is the missing link that resolves the paradox concerning character—when your face in the world and worldliness are for the time put aside, when you disregard the effect your work will have, one way or the other, on the public. To make good art—and again this applies to the beholder—you have to go where you have to go. There are no certainties and no guarantees—only risks and they must be taken.

9. Statement on Olitski's Dance Floor *for Harvard University, which now exists as a model (pl. 229). Feb. 18, 1981.*

The dance floor has multi-levels. In actual construction, it would be built in sections with rollers under each section, so that the "floor" could be rapidly assembled, with each section interlocking—hence, the jig-saw puzzle-like drawing upon the face of the model. A dance would begin with each section being rolled into place and interlocked, until finally the entire floor was assembled. The dance could begin at any point during this process, or after the whole floor was in place. The other purpose of designing in sections has to do with facilitating disassembly of the dance floor, storage (one section can be laid on top of another, and so on), as well as transporting the dance floor from one place to another.

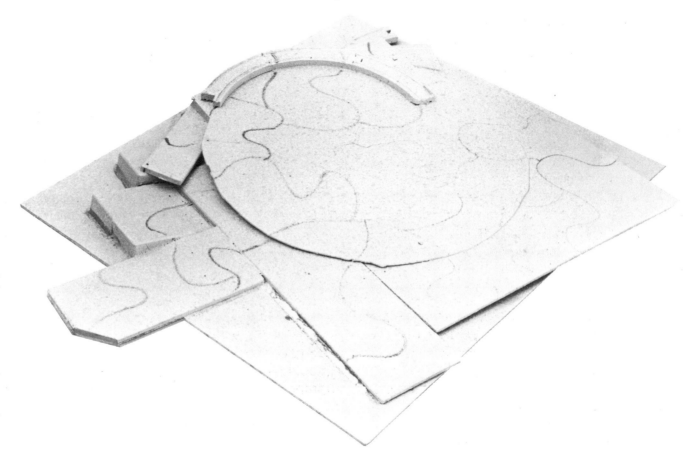

229. Model of *Dance Floor* for Harvard University, Cambridge, Mass. Collection of the artist

---

* Said to me in conversation by Clement Greenberg.

SELECTED EXHIBITIONS

1961

"The 1961 Pittsburgh International Exhibition of Contemporary Painting and Sculpture," Department of Fine Arts, Carnegie Institute, Pittsburgh, Pa., Oct. 27, 1961–Jan. 7, 1962. Awarded second prize for *Osculum Silence*. Catalogue, with introduction by Gordon Bailey Washburn. (One painting: *Osculum Silence*.)

1962

"Jules Olitski," New Gallery, Bennington College, Vt., Oct.-Nov. Organized by Paul Feeley. (Six paintings: *Green Jazz, Purple Passion Company, Sacred Courtesans Blue, Pink Love, Yellow Juice, Ino Delight*.)

"Recent Acquisitions," The Museum of Modern Art, New York, Nov. 20, 1962–Jan. 3, 1963. Checklist. (One painting: *Cleopatra Flesh*.)

"Whitney Annual Exhibition of Contemporary American Painting," Whitney Museum of American Art, New York, Dec. 11, 1962–Feb. 2, 1963. Catalogue. (One painting: *Queen of Sheba Breast*.)

1963

"Three New American Painters: Louis, Noland, Olitski," Norman Mackenzie Art Gallery, University of Saskatchewan, Regina, Sask., Jan. 11–Feb. 15. Catalogue, with introduction by Clement Greenberg (reprinted in *Canadian Art*, May 1963, pp. 172–75). (Three paintings: *Green Jazz, Purple Passion Company, Ino Delight*.)

"Aspects of 20th Century Painting," Worcester Art Museum, Worcester, Mass., Feb. 7–Apr. 7. Checklist. (One painting: *Cadmium Orange of Dr. Frankenstein*.)

"The Formalists," Washington Gallery of Modern Art, Washington, D.C., June 6–July 7. Catalogue. (Two paintings: *Isis Ardor, Yaksi Juice*.)

"Directions: American Painting," San Francisco Museum of Art, San Francisco, Sept. 20–Oct. 20. Checklist. (One painting: *Mushroom Perfume*.)

"New Directions in American Painting," organized by the Rose Art Museum, Brandeis University, Waltham, Mass. Exhibited at Munson-Williams-Proctor Institute, Utica, N. Y., Dec. 1, 1963–Jan. 5, 1964; Isaac Delgado Museum of Art, New Orleans, La., Feb. 7–Mar. 8, 1964; Atlanta Art Association, Atlanta, Ga., Mar. 18–Apr. 22, 1964; J.B. Speed Art Museum, Louisville, Ky., May 4–June 7, 1964; Art Museum, Indiana University, Bloomington, Ind., June 22–Sept. 20, 1964; Washington University, St. Louis, Mo., Oct. 5–30, 1964; Detroit Institute of Arts, Detroit, Mich., Nov. 10–Dec. 6, 1964. Catalogue, with introduction by Sam Hunter. (One painting: *Yaksi Juice*.)

1964

"67th Annual American Exhibition," Art Institute of Chicago, Chicago, Feb. 28–Apr. 12. Catalogue. (Two paintings: *Equator Crossing, Born in Snovsk*.)

"The Atmosphere of 1964," Institute of Contemporary Art, University of Pennsylvania, Philadelphia, Apr. 17–June 1. Checklist. (Four paintings: *Butterfly Kiss, Doozhie Orgy, Flaming Passion of Beverly Torrid, Beautiful Bald Woman*.)

"Post Painterly Abstraction," Los Angeles County Museum of Art, Los Angeles, Apr. 23–June 7; Walker Art Center, Minneapolis, Minn., July 13–Aug. 16; Art Gallery of Toronto, Toronto, Ont. Nov. 20–Dec. 20. Catalogue, with introduction by Clement Greenberg (reprinted in *Art International*, Summer 1964, pp. 63–65). (Three paintings: *Isis Ardor, Mushroom Perfume, Julius Caesar in Egypt*.)

"American Drawings, 1964," The Solomon R. Guggenheim Museum, New York, Sept. 17–Oct. 27. Catalogue, with introduction by Lawrence Alloway. (Four pastels on paper, all untitled.)

1965

"Three American Painters (Noland, Olitski and Stella)," Fogg Art Museum, Harvard University, Cambridge, Mass., Apr. 21–May 30; Pasadena Art Museum, Pasadena, Calif., July 6–Aug. 3. Catalogue, with introduction by Michael Fried. (Six paintings: *Deep Drag, Flaming On, Flaubert Red, Hot Ticket, Tin Lizzy Green, Strip Heresy*.)

"Ausstellung Signale," Kunsthalle, Basel, Switzerland, June 26–Sept. 5. Catalogue. (Seven paintings: *Prince Patutsky Red, Green Jazz, Chemise, Green Love Game, Untitled, Small Black Painting, One Time Rectangle*.)

1966

"Frankenthaler, Noland, Olitski," New Brunswick Museum, St. John, N. B.; Norman Mackenzie Art Gallery, University of Saskatchewan, Regina, Sask.; The Mendel Art Center, Saskatoon, Sask.; Confederation Art Gallery and Museum, Charlottetown, Prince Edward Island. Catalogue, with introduction by Barry J. Lord. (Five paintings: *Zem Zem, Tea Party, Harlow Flow, Temptations, Monday Night Mark*.)

"XXXIII International Biennial Exhibition of Art," United States Pavilion, Venice, Italy, June 18–Oct. 16. Catalogue, with introduction by Henry Geldzahler, essay by Clement Greenberg. Remarks by the artist (reprinted, slightly revised, in *Artforum*, Jan. 1967, p. 20). (Seven paintings: *Lovely Scream, Of Gomel, One Eight Six, Prince Patutsky's Command, Thigh Smoke, Unlocked, Vertical*.)

1967

"30th Biennial Exhibition of Contemporary American Painting," Corcoran Gallery of Art, Washington, D.C. (Award: Corcoran Gold Medal and William A. C. Clark Prize), Feb. 24–Apr. 19. Catalogue. (Four paintings: *Exact Origin, Frame Expansion, Pink Alert, Sleep Robber*.)

"Form, Color, Image," Detroit Institute of Arts, Detroit, Mich., Apr. 11–May 21. Catalogue, with introduction by Gene Baro. (Three paintings: *Deep Suze, Summer, Thigh Smoke*.)

"Ninth Tokyo Biennale," Tokyo, Japan, May. Catalogue. (One painting: *Galliloo*.)

"A Selection of Paintings and Sculptures from the Collections of Mr. and Mrs. Robert Rowan," University of California, Irvine, May 2–21; San Francisco Museum of Art, San Francisco, June 2–July 2. Checklist. (Eight paintings: *Julius Orange, Prince Patutsky in Bennington, Arnolfini Baby, Deep Drag, Flaming On, Purple Casanova, Beatrice Blue, Juice*.)

"Focus on Light," New Jersey State Museum, Trenton, May 20–Sept. 10. Catalogue, with introduction by Lucy R. Lippard. (One painting: *Prinkep*.)

"Large-Scale American Paintings," The Jewish Museum, New York, July 11–Sept. 17. Checklist. (One painting: *Magic Number*.)

"Torcuato di Tella International Prize Exhibition," Istituto Torcuato di Tella, Buenos Aires, Argentina, Sept. 29–Oct. 29. Catalogue. (One painting: *Thigh Smoke*.)

"Art for Embassies," Organized by the Washington Gallery of Modern Art, Washington, D. C., Sept. 30–Nov. 5. Catalogue, with introduction by

Henry Geldzahler. (One painting: *Turkey Girl*.)

"Jules Olitski: Paintings 1963–1967," Corcoran Gallery of Art, Washington, D.C., Apr. 28–June 11; Pasadena Art Museum, Pasadena, Calif., Aug. 1–Sept. 10; San Francisco Museum of Art, San Francisco, Sept. 26–Nov. 5. Catalogue, with introduction by Michael Fried. (Forty-four paintings.)

"Whitney Annual Exhibition of Contemporary American Painting," Whitney Museum of American Art, New York, Dec. 13, 1967–Feb. 4, 1968. Catalogue. (One painting. *Pink Tinge*.)

1968

"Jules Olitski; Recent Paintings," Institute of Contemporary Art, University of Pennsylvania, Philadelphia, Feb. 21–Mar. 26, in collaboration with the Hayden Gallery, Massachusetts Institute of Technology, Cambridge, Mar. 29–Apr. 23. Catalogue, with introduction by Rosalind E. Krauss. (Seventeen paintings.)

"Documenta IV," Kassel, Germany, June 27–Oct. 6. Catalogue, with essay by Jean Leering. (Two paintings: *Tender Boogus, Instant Loveland*.)

"Signals in the Sixties," Honolulu Academy of Arts, Honolulu, Hawaii, Oct. 5–Nov. 10. Catalogue, with introduction by James Johnson Sweeney. (One painting: *C + J&B*.)

"L'Art Vivant, 1965–1968," Fondation Maeght, St. Paul-de-Vence, France, Apr. 13–June 30. Catalogue, with introduction by François Wehrlin. (One painting: *Vabo*.)

"Albert Pilavin Collection: Twentieth-Century American Art," Rhode Island School of Design Museum, Providence, R. I., Oct. 7–Nov. 23. Catalogue (*Bulletin of the Rhode Island School of Design*.) (One painting: *Sensay*.)

1969

"Selections from the Richard Brown Baker Collection," Art Gallery, University of Notre Dame, Ind., Jan. 5–Feb. 23. Catalogue. (One painting: *Queen of Sheba Breast*.)

"The Development of Modernist Painting: Jackson Pollock to the Present," Steinberg Art Gallery, Washington University Gallery of Art, St. Louis, Mo., Apr. 1–30. Catalogue, with introduction by Robert T. Buck, Jr. (One painting: *Free and Fast*.)

"The Sculpture of Jules Olitski," The Metropolitan Museum of Art, New York, Apr. 10–May 18. Essay by Kenworth Moffett, *The Metropolitan Museum of Art Bulletin*, Apr. 1969, pp. 336–71 (revised version in *Artforum*, Apr. 1969, pp. 55–59). Statement by Olitski, "On Sculpture," *The Metropolitan Museum of Art Bulletin*, Apr. 1969 (reprinted in *Art Now: New York*, May 1969). (Six sculptures: *Whip-out, Heartbreak of Ronald and William, Six-banger, Wheels-up, Whipsaw, Ohel of Volya*.)

"Concept," Vassar College Art Gallery, Poughkeepsie, N.Y., Apr. 30–June 1. Catalogue, with "Some Observations on Concept" by Mary Delahoyd. (One painting: *Gearing Up*.)

"The Gosman Collection," Art Gallery of the University of Pittsburgh, Department of Fine Arts, Pittsburgh, Pa., Sept. 14–Oct. 10. Catalogue, with essay by Aaron Sheon. (One painting: *Inside Voyage*.)

"American Art of the 60's: Toronto Private Collections," York University, Toronto, Ont. Catalogue, with foreword by Michael Greenwood. (Two paintings: *Harlow Flow, Fourth Caliph*.)

"Contemporary American Painting and Sculpture from the Collection of Mr. and Mrs. Eugene M. Schwartz, Everson Museum of Art, Syracuse, N.Y.,

July 13–Nov. 16; University Art Gallery, State University of New York at Albany, Dec. 3, 1969–Jan. 25, 1970. Catalogue. (Two paintings: *Strip Heresy, Shake Up*.)

"New York Painting and Sculpture: 1940–1970," The Metropolitan Museum of Art, New York, Oct. 18, 1969–Feb. 8, 1970. Catalogue, with introduction by Henry Geldzahler. (Eight paintings: *Ten O'Clock, Bathsheba, Ritual of L, Commissar Demikovsky, Thigh Smoke, Disarmed, Green Valya, Warehouse Lights*; one sculpture: *Twelve Nights*.)

"Painting in New York: 1944–1969," Pasadena Art Museum, Pasadena, Calif., Nov. 24, 1969–Jan. 11, 1970. Catalogue, with "Some Observations about New York Painting" by Alan Solomon. (Three paintings: *Flaming On, Susie Wiles, Prince Patutsky in Bennington*.)

"1969 Annual Exhibition of Contemporary American Painting," Whitney Museum of American Art, New York, Dec. 16, 1969–Feb. 1, 1970. Catalogue. (One painting: *Embrace*)

1970

"69th Annual American Exhibition," Art Institute of Chicago, Chicago, Jan. 17–Feb. 22. Catalogue. (Two paintings: *Outrider, Goozler*.)

"American Artists of the Nineteen-Sixties." Centennial Exhibition, Boston University, School of Fine and Applied Arts, Boston, Feb. 6–Mar. 14. Catalogue, with essay by H. Harvard Arnason. (One painting: *Main Squeeze*.)

"Color," UCLA Art Galleries, Los Angeles, Feb. 15–Mar. 22. Catalogue, with essay on Jules Olitski by Lynn Bailess and Carol Donnell. (Four paintings: *Optimum, Surface Scrambler, Untitled, EE*; one sculpture: *Bunga 45*.)

"Contemporary Painting and Sculpture," Wellesley College Museum, Jewett Art Center, Wellesley, Mass., Mar. 7–Apr. 26. Catalogue. (Three paintings: *Beyond Bounds, Paid Model, Green Hands*; one sculpture: *Whipsaw*.)

"Giant Images of Today," Everson Museum of Art, Syracuse, N.Y., Aug. 15–Sept. 30. Catalogue. (One painting: *Disarmed*.)

"35th Annual Exhibition," Butler Institute of American Art, Youngstown, Ohio, June 28–Aug. 30. (One painting: *Masker*.)

"Two Generations of Color Painting," Institute of Contemporary Art, University of Pennsylvania, Philadelphia, Oct. 1–Nov. 6. Catalogue, with introduction by Stephen S. Prokopoff. (One painting: *Green Marfak*.)

"Selections from the Mr. and Mrs. Robert A. Rowan Collection," Pasadena Art Museum, Pasadena, Calif., Nov. 15, 1970. Checklist. (Six paintings: *Juice, Comprehensive Dream, Deep Drag, Arnolfini Baby, Drakely, Tender Boogus*.)

"Painting and Sculpture Today," Contemporary Art Society and Indianapolis Museum of Art, Indianapolis, Ind. Catalogue, with introduction by Richard L. Warrum. (One painting: *Secret Pearlessence*.)

"Color and Field: 1890–1970," Albright-Knox Art Gallery, Buffalo, N. Y., Sept. 15–Nov. 1; Dayton Art Institute, Dayton, Ohio, Nov. 20, 1970–Jan. 10, 1971; Cleveland Museum of Art, Cleveland, Ohio, Feb. 4–Mar. 28, 1971. Catalogue, with introduction by Priscilla Colt. (Four paintings: *Commissar Demikovsky, Intimacy, Main Squeeze, 29th Hope*.)

"The Drawing Society National Exhibition, 1970," circulating exhibition, 1970–72. Catalogue, with introduction by James Biddle, "Thoughts on

Drawing'' by Robert Motherwell. (One pencil drawing: *Nude III*.)

1971

"Contemporary American Painting and Sculpture: Selections from the Collection of Mr. and Mrs. Eugene M. Schwartz," Milwaukee Art Center, Milwaukee, Wisc., Jan. 22–Feb. 28. Catalogue, with introduction by Carl Schmalz. (Three paintings: *Shake Up, Strip Heresy, Short*.)

"The Structure of Color," Whitney Museum of American Art, New York, Feb. 25–Apr. 18. Catalogue, with essay by Marcia Tucker, statement by the artist. (One painting: *3rd Indomitable*.)

"Jules Olitski," University of Michigan Museum of Art, Ann Arbor, Mich., Apr. 11–May 9. Checklist, with statement by the artist ("Painting in Color," reprinted from *Artforum*, Jan. 1967). (Seven paintings: *10th Loosha, 3rd Loosha, 2nd Indomitable, Front Breaker #2, Goozler, Female Shiver, EE*.)

"The Deluxe Show," sponsored by the Ménil Foundation, Houston, Tex., Aug. 15–Sept. 12. Catalogue, with introduction by Steve Cannon; interview with Clement Greenberg by Simone Swan. (One painting: *Loosha One*.)

"The Vincent Melzac Collection," Corcoran Gallery of Art, Washington, D.C. Catalogue, with introduction by Ellen Gross Landau, retrospective notes on the Washington School by Barbara Rose. (One painting: *Cadmium Orange of Dr. Frankenstein*.)

"Spray," The Santa Barbara Museum of Art, Santa Barbara, Calif. Catalogue, with introduction by Paul C. Mills.

1972

"Whitney Annual Exhibition of Contemporary American Painting," Whitney Museum of American Art, New York, Jan. 25–Mar. 19. Catalogue. (One painting: *Irkutsk Dawn*.)

"Color Painting," Amherst College, Amherst, Mass., Feb. 4–Mar. 3. (One painting: *Irkutsk*.)

"Abstract Painting in the 70's: A Selection," Museum of Fine Arts, Boston, Apr. 14–May 21. Catalogue, with introduction by Kenworth Moffett. (Four paintings: *3rd Indomitable, 8th Loosha, Orange Hook, Omsk Measure*.)

"Masters of the Sixties," Edmonton Art Gallery, Edmonton, Alta., May 4–June 4. Catalogue, with introduction by Karen Wilkin. (One painting: *Goozler*; one sculpture: *St. Neots Night*.)

"Twentieth Century Prints from the Dartmouth College Collection," compiled by members of the History of Prints Seminar, Department of Art, Hanover, N.H., May 19–July 9. (One silkscreen: *Untitled, 1970*.)

"Contemporary Art: The Collection of Dr. and Mrs. Joseph Gosman," University of Michigan Museum of Art, Ann Arbor, Mich., Sept. 13–Oct. 15. Catalogue. (One painting: *Inside Voyage*.)

"Color Field Paintings to Post Color Field Abstraction—Art for the 70's," Nelson Gallery-Atkins Museum, Kansas City, Mo.

1973

"Jules Olitski," Museum of Fine Arts, Boston, Apr. 6–May 13; Albright-Knox Art Gallery, Buffalo, N.Y., May 31–July 29; Whitney Museum of American Art, New York, Sept. 7–Nov. 4. Catalogue, with introduction by Kenworth Moffett, chronology by Elinor Woron. (57 paintings.)

"Maîtres de l'Abstraction Americaine Aujourd'hui," Galerie Daniel Templon, Paris, France, summer.

"Prospect '73," Düsseldorf, West Germany, Sept. (One painting: *Divine Hostage 2*, 1973.)

1974

"The Great Decade of American Abstraction, Modernist Art 1960 to 1970," Museum of Fine Arts, Houston, Tex., Jan. 15–Mar. 10. Catalogue, with introduction by E.A. Carmean. (Five paintings: *Born in Snovsk*, 1963; *Flaubert Red*, 1964; *Intimacy*, 1965; *Mojo Working*, 1966; *Main Squeeze*, 1969.)

"Jules Olitski, Life Drawings," Corcoran Gallery of Art, Washington, D.C., Feb. 9–Mar. 10. Traveled to Winnepeg Art Gallery, Winnepeg, Man.; Norman Mackenzie Art Gallery, Regina, Sask.; Edmonton Art Gallery, Edmonton, Alta.; Art Gallery of Ontario, Toronto; Art Gallery of Hamilton, Hamilton, Ont.; Art Gallery of Windsor, Windsor, Ont.; Musée d'Art Contemporain, Montreal, Que.; Weatherspoon Art Gallery, Greensboro, N.C.; Hunter Museum of Art, Chattanooga, Tenn. Catalogue, with introduction by Andrew Hudson.

"Selections from the Collection of Carter Burden," Marlborough Gallery, New York, May 9–June 1.. (One painting: *Z*, 1964.)

"Painting and Sculpture Today 1974," Indianapolis Museum of Art, Indianapolis, Ind., May 22–July 14; Taft Museum, Cincinnati, Ohio, Sept. 12–Oct. 26. Catalogue. (One painting: *Overtone One*, 1970.)

"Daniel Templon, L'Art au Present," Palais Galliera, Paris, France, Oct. 2–Nov. 10.

"Selections from the Collections of Mr. and Mrs. Robert A. Rowan," Santa Barbara Museum of Art, Santa Barbara, Calif., Nov. 2–24. (Four paintings: *Arnolfini Baby*, 1964; *Drakely*, 1966; *Juice*, 1966; *Other Flesh 8*, 1972.)

1975

"The Virginia and Bagley Wright Collection, American Art Since 1960," Denver Art Museum, Denver, Colo., Feb. 1–Mar. 16. Catalogue, with introduction by Thomas N. Maytham. (One painting: *Pink Tinge*, 1967.)

"34th Biennial of Contemporary American Painting," Corcoran Gallery of Art, Washington, D.C., Feb. 22–Apr. 6. (One painting: *Areteas Replies—3*, 1974.)

"Richard Brown Baker Collects," Yale University Art Gallery, New Haven, Conn., Apr. 24–June 22. (One painting: *Queen of Sheba Breast*.)

"El Lenguaje del Color," Museo de Bellas Artes, Caracas, Venezuela, Aug. Exhibition under the auspices of the International Council of The Museum of Modern Art of New York and La Sociedad Amigos del Museo de Bellas Artes de Caracas.

"Monumenta," Newport, R. I., Aug. 17–Oct. 13. An outdoor exhibition of sculpture. Catalogue, with introduction by Sam Hunter. (One sculpture: *Chinese Cassandra*.)

1976

"New Works in Clay," Everson Museum of Art, Syracuse, N.Y., Jan. 24–Apr. 4. Catalogue, with introduction by Marjorie Hughto. (Fourteen works, all done in Syracuse.)

"Jules Olitski," Galleria Civica, Modena, Italy, Mar. 18–May 2.

"American Color: 1961–1964," School of Visual Arts, New York, Mar. 29–Apr. 21. Catalogue, with essay by Jeanne Siegel. (One painting: *Tin Lizzy Green*, 1964.)

"Painting and Sculpture Today 1976," Indianapolis Museum of Art, Indianapolis, Ind., June 9–July 18. Catalogue. (One painting: *Third Dooja*, 1974.)

"The Hue and Far Cry of Color," Museum of Art, Fort Wayne Art Institute, Ind., May 1–30. (One painting: *Habakkuk Radiance #22*, 1973.)

1977

"Olitski, New Sculpture," Museum of Fine Arts, Boston, Apr. 26–July 3; Hirshhorn Museum and Sculpture Garden, Washington, D.C., July 20–Oct. 2. Catalogue, with introduction by Kenworth Moffett, interview with artist by Friedrich Bach. (Six sculptures: *Greenberg Variations, Also Admah, Shechinah Temptations, Ur, Lippis de Salomé, Réjane Possessed*.)

"A View of a Decade," Museum of Contemporary Art, Chicago, Sept. 10–Nov. 10. Catalogue, with essays by Martin Friedman, Robert Pincus-Witten, and Peter Gay. (One painting: *Pleasure Ground #1*.)

"Critics' Choice, A Loan Exhibition of Contemporary Painting from the New York Gallery Season, 1976–77," Joe and Emily Lowe Art Gallery, Syracuse University, Syracuse, N.Y., Nov. 13–Dec. 11; Munson-Williams-Proctor Institute, Utica, N.Y., Jan. 3–30, 1978. Painting by Olitski chosen by the critic Thomas Hess. Catalogue, with essays by Gene Baro, Hayden Herrera, Thomas Hess, and Carter Ratcliff. (One painting: *Heraclitus Step I*, 1968.)

1978

"One Century: Wellesley Families Collect, an Exhibition Celebrating the Centennial of Wellesley College," Wellesley College, Wellesley, Mass., Apr. 15–May 30. Catalogue, with introduction by Ann Gabhardt and Judith Hoos Fox.

"Fifteen Sculptors in Steel Around Bennington 1963–1978," Park-McCullough House Association, North Bennington, Vt., Aug. 12–Oct. 15. Catalogue, with introduction by Andrew Hudson. (Three sculptures: *King Kong*, 1973; *Ur*, 1976, *Lippis de Salomé*, 1977.)

"American Painting of the 1970's," Albright-Knox Art Gallery, Buffalo, N.Y., Dec. 8, 1978–Jan. 14, 1979; Newport Harbor Art Museum, Newport Beach, Calif., Feb. 3–Mar. 8, 1979; Oakland Art Museum, Oakland, Calif., Apr. 10–May 20, 1979; Cincinnati Art Museum, Cincinnati, Ohio, July 6–Aug. 26, 1979; Art Museum of South Texas, Corpus Christi, Tex., Sept. 9–Oct. 21, 1979; Krannert Art Museum, University of Illinois, Champaign, Ill., Nov. 11, 1979–Jan. 2, 1980. Catalogue, with introduction by Linda L. Cathcart. (One painting: *Line Passage I*, 1977.)

1979

"Jules Olitski: Paintings of the 1970s," Edmonton Art Gallery, Edmonton, Alta., Sept. 12–Oct. 28. Catalogue, with introduction by Terry Fenton entitled "Jules Olitski and the Tradition of Oil Painting."

"Color Abstractions: Selections from the Museum of Fine Arts, Boston," Federal Reserve Bank of Boston, Nov. 2, 1979–Mar. 14, 1980. Catalogue, with introduction by Kenworth Moffett. (One painting: *Tin Lizzy Green*, 1964.)

1980

"Morton G. Neuman Family Collection," National Gallery of Art, Washington, D.C., Oct. 31–Dec. 31. Catalogue, with text by E. A. Carmean, Trinkett Clark, and Eliza E. Rathbone. (One painting: *Laramop—2*.)

1981

"Depuis la couleur 1958–64," CAPC, Bordeaux, France, Jan. 23–Mar. 21.

"International Florida Artists," Ringling Museum, Sarasota, Fla., Feb. 26–Apr. 26.

SELECTED MUSEUM COLLECTIONS

The Metropolitan Museum of Art, New York
The Museum of Modern Art, New York
Museum of Fine Arts, Boston
Solomon R. Guggenheim Museum, New York
Whitney Museum of American Art, New York
Brooklyn Museum, New York
Art Institute of Chicago
Hirshhorn Museum and Sculpture Garden, Washington, D.C.
National Gallery of Art, Washington, D.C.
Pasadena Art Museum, Pasadena, California
Seattle Art Museum, Seattle, Washington
Detroit Institute of Arts, Detroit, Michigan
National Gallery of Canada, Ottawa, Ontario
Dayton Art Institute, Dayton, Ohio
Albright-Knox Art Gallery, Buffalo, New York
Edmonton Art Gallery, Edmonton, Alberta
Everson Museum of Art, Syracuse, New York
Fogg Art Museum, Harvard University, Cambridge, Massachusetts
Corcoran Gallery of Art, Washington, D.C.
Dallas Museum of Fine Arts, Dallas, Texas
Museum of Fine Arts, Houston, Texas
Milwaukee Art Center, Milwaukee, Wisconsin
University of Michigan Museum of Art, Ann Arbor, Michigan
Art Museum, Princeton University, Princeton, New Jersey
Nelson Gallery-Atkins Museum, Kansas City, Missouri
Storm King Art Center, Mountainville, New York
Art Collection of Nordrhein-Westfalen, Düsseldorf, West Germany
The Israel Museum, Jerusalem, Israel
Natonal Gallery of Australia, Canberra

SELECTED BIBLIOGRAPHY

1959

Campbell, Lawrence. "Jules Olitski." *Art News*, May, p. 50.

Preston, Stuart. "Three Generations of Moderns." *The New York Times,* May 24, p. 17.

Tillim, Sidney, "Jules Olitski," *Arts Magazine,* June, p. 56.

1961

Canaday, John. "International Exhibition Opens in Pittsburgh." *The New York Times,* Oct. 27, p. 66.

1963

Greenberg, Clement. *Three New American Painters: Louis, Noland, Olitski.* Catalogue introduction. Regina, Sask.: Norman Mackenzie Art Gallery. (Reprinted in *Canadian Art,* May 1963, pp. 172–75.)

Hudson, Andrew. "Art." *The Nor'wester,* Saskatoon, Jan. 17.

———. "On Looking at the New Paintings." *Regina Saskatoon Review,* Aug. 5.

1964

Fried, Michael. "New York Letter." *Art International,* May, pp. 40–42.

Greenberg, Clement. *Post Painterly Abstraction.* Catalogue introduction. Los Angeles: Los Angeles County Museum of Art (Reprinted in *Art International,* Summer 1964, pp. 63–65.)

1965

Fried, Michael. "Jules Olitski's New Paintings." *Artforum,* Nov., pp. 36–40.

———, *Three American Painters: Noland, Olitski, and Stella.* Catalogue introduction. Cambridge, Mass.: Fogg Art Museum.

Hudson, Andrew. "Viewpoint on Art." *Washington Post,* Oct. 31, p. G-7.

Kozloff, Max. "Frankenthaler and Olit-ski." *The Nation,* Apr., pp. 374–76.

Lippard, Lucy R. "New York Letter." *Art International,* May, p. 55.

Lynton, Norbert. "London Letter." *Art International,* Sept., p. 50.

Rose, Barbara. "The Second Generation: Academy and Breakthrough." *Artforum,* Sept., pp. 53–62.

1966

Fried, Michael. "Shape as Form: Frank Stella's New Paintings." *Artforum,* Nov., pp. 18–27.

Geldzahler, Henry. "Frankenthaler, Kelly, Lichtenstein, Olitski: A Preview of the American Selection at the 1966 Venice Biennale." *Artforum,* June, pp. 32–38.

Greenberg, Clement. "Jules Olitski," in *XXXIII International Biennial Exhibition of Art.* Venice.

Hudson, Andrew. "New York Shows Reveal Artists on the Rise—and in Decline." *Washington Post,* Nov. 6, p. G-9.

———. "Biennial Begins Season—At Last," *Washington Post,* Dec. 4, p. G-1.

———. "Viewpoint on Art." *Washington Post,* Dec. 25, p. G-9.

Kramer, Hilton. "Art: (Jules Olitski.)" *The New York Times,* Nov. 5, p. 26.

Lippard, Lucy R. "New York Letter." *Art International,* Jan., pp. 90–91.

Lord, Barry J. *Frankenthaler, Noland, Olitski.* Catalogue introduction. St. John: New Brunswick Museum.

———. "Three American Painters Tour Canada." *Canadian Art,* July, p. 50.

Meadmore, Clement. "New York Scene II: Color as an Idiom." *Art and Australia,* Mar., pp. 288–91.

Mellow, James R. "New York Letter." *Art International,* Dec., pp. 61–64.

Millen, Ronald. "Fun and Games in Venice." *Art and Australia,* Nov., p. 41.

Olitski, Jules. "Painting in Color," in *XXXIII International Biennial Exhibition of Art.* Venice.

Scott, David. "America's Role in the Biennale." *The Art Gallery,* June, p. 10.

Solomon, Alan. "American Art between Two Biennales." *Metro II,* Spring.

———. "The Green Mountain Boys." *Vogue,* Aug., pp. 104–109, 151–52.

Volpi, Marisa. "Qui U.S.A.: Biennale in Anteprima." *La Fiera Letteraria,* June.

1967

Baro, Gene. "Washington and Detroit." *Studio International,* July–Aug., pp. 49–51.

———. *Form, Color, Image.* Catalogue introduction. Detroit, Mich.: Detroit Institute of Arts.

Champa, Kermit S. "Olitski: Nothing but Color." *Art News,* May, pp. 36–38, 74–76.

———. "Albert Stadler: New Paintings." *Artforum,* Sept., pp. 30–34.

Feldman, Anita. "In the Museums: Large Scale American Paintings." *Arts Magazine,* Sept.–Oct., p. 52.

———. "In the Galleries." *Arts Magazine,* Dec. 1967–Jan. 1968, p. 58.

Fried, Michael. "Olitski and Shape." *Artforum,* Jan., pp. 20–21.

———. *Jules Olitski, Paintings 1963–1967.* Catalogue introduction. Washington, D.C.: Corcoran Gallery of Art.

———. "Ronald Davis: Surface and Illusion." *Artforum,* Apr., pp. 37–41.

———. "Art and Objecthood." *Artforum,* Summer, pp. 12–23.

Hudson, Andrew. "Biennial is a Four Star Show." *Washington Post,* Mar. 5, p. F-8.

———. "A Painter Breaks New Ground." *Washington Post,* Apr. 9, p. H-8.

———. "Washington: An 'American Salon' of 1967." *Art International,* Apr., pp. 73–79.

———. "Shows are Rich in Comparison." *Washington Post,* May 21, p. H-8.

———. "The 1967 Pittsburgh International." *Art International,* Christmas, pp. 57–64.

Kozloff, Max. "New York," *Artforum,* Dec., p. 52.

Kramer, Hilton. "Art: Corcoran Prizes No Surprises." *The New York Times,* Feb. 24, p. 32.

Lippard, Lucy R. *Focus on Light.* Catalogue introduction. Trenton: New Jersey State Museum.

McQuillan, Melissa. "New York Reviews." *Harvard Art Review,* Winter, pp. 49–50.

Mellow, James R. "New York Letter." *Art International,* Christmas, pp. 72–73.

Olitski, Jules. "Painting in Color," *Artforum,* Jan., p. 20 (slightly revised and expanded version of Olitski's statement in *XXXIII International Biennial Exhibition of Art,* Venice, June 1966).

Pincus-Witten, Robert. "New York." *Artforum,* Dec., pp. 52–53.

Rose, Barbara. "Abstract Illusionism." *Artforum,* Oct., pp. 33–37.

———. "Washington Scene." *Artforum,* Nov., pp. 56–57.

Rosenberg, Harold. "The Art World." *The New Yorker,* Aug., pp. 90, 93–97.

Tillim, Sidney. "Scale and the Future of Modernism." *Artforum,* Oct., pp. 14–18.

Von Meier, Kurt. "Los Angeles." *Art International,* Oct., pp. 57–59.

1968

Burton, Scott. "Reviews and Previews: Jules Olitski at Poindexter Gallery." *Art News,* Feb., p. 15.

Danelli, Fidel. "Jules Olitski." *Art Digest Newsletter,* Nov. 1, p. 5.

Donohoe, Victoria. "King size Paintings Surging with Color." *The Philadelphia Inquirer,* Feb. 25.

Driscoll, Edgar, Jr. "Artist Romero Opens New Gallery." *The Boston Globe,* Apr. 2, p. 20.

Glueck, Grace. "Alone at Last—with a Trend." *The New York Times,* Dec. 1, p. 41.

Gouk, Alan. "Apropos of Some Recent Exhibitions in London." *Studio International,* Oct., pp. 125–26.

Grafly, Dorothy. "Diverse Styles Reflect the Vast and the Intimate." *Philadelphia Bulletin,* Feb. 25.

Harrison, Charles. "London Commentaries: Jules Olitski at the Kasmin Gallery." *Studio International,* Sept., pp. 86–87.

Hudson, Andrew. "On Jules Olitski's Paintings and Some Changes of View." *Art International,* Jan., pp. 31–36.

Krauss, Rosalind E. *Jules Olitski: Recent Paintings.* Catalogue introduction. Philadelphia: Institute of Contemporary Art, University of Pennsylvania.

———. "On Frontality." *Artforum,* May, pp. 40–46.

Kudielka, Robert. "Documenta 4: A Critical Review." *Studio International,* Sept., p. 78.

Leering, Jean. "Post Painterly Abstraction," in *Documenta IV,* Kassel, Germany.

Nemser, Cindy. "In the Galleries: Jules Olitski." *Arts Magazine,* Dec. 1968–Jan. 1969, p. 63.

"Olitski Show Opens U. of P. Arts Building." *Sunday Bulletin* (Philadelphia), Feb. 18.

Perreault, John. "Art: Jules Olitski." *The Village Voice,* Nov. 28, p. 19.

Sweeney, James J. *Signals in the '60s.* Catalogue introduction. Honolulu, Hawaii: Honolulu Academy of Arts.

Tillim, Sidney. "Evaluations and Re-evaluations: A Season's End Miscellany." *Artforum,* Summer, pp. 20–23.

1969

Ashton, Dore. "Esempi recenti di pittura non oggttiva negli Stati Uniti." *L'Arte moderna,* vol. 13, pp. 94, 114.

———. "New York Commentary." *Studio International,* July–Aug., p. 28.

Buck, Robert T., Jr. *The Development of Modernist Painting: Jackson Pollock to the Present.* Catalogue introduction. St. Louis, Mo.: Steinberg Gallery of Art, Washington University.

Campbell, Lawrence. "Reviews and Previews." *Art News,* Dec., p. 69.

Canaday, John. "Pleased Here, Puzzled There." *The New York Times,* Dec. 25, p. 25.

Chisholm, Shirley. "Jules Olitski." *Current Biography,* Oct., pp. 31–34.

Delahoyd, Mary. "Some Observations on Concept," in *Concept.* Poughkeepsie, N.Y.: Vassar College Art Gallery.

Feldman, Anita. "In the Galleries." *Arts Magazine,* Dec. 1969–Jan. 1970, p. 68.

Greenwood, Michael. *American Art of the Sixties in Toronto: Private Collections.* Catalogue introduction. Toronto, Ont.: York University.

Kramer, Hilton. "Sculpture: The Debut of Jules Olitski." *The New York Times,* Apr. 12, p. 31.

Kurtz, Stephen A. "Reviews and Previews: Jules Olitski." *Art News,* Jan., p. 25.

Mellow, James R. "New York Letter." *Art International,* Summer, p. 51.

Moffett, Kenworth. "The Sculpture of Jules Olitski." *The Metropolitan Museum of Art Bulletin,* Apr., pp. 336–71. (Revised and reprinted in *Artforum,* Apr., pp. 55–59.)

Olitski, Jules. "On Sculpture." *The Metropolitan Museum of Art Bulletin,* Apr., p. 366. (Reprinted in *Art Now: New York,* May, n.p.)

Platt, Susan. "Notes on the Albert Pilavin Collection: Twentieth-Century American Art." *Bulletin of the Rhode Island School of Design,* Summer, pp. 37–39.

Schjeldahl, Peter. "New York Letter." *Art International,* Summer, p. 64.

Sheon, Aaron. *The Gosman Collection.* Catalogue introduction. Pittsburgh, Pa.: Art Gallery of the University of Pittsburgh, Department of Fine Arts.

Shirey, David L. "New York Painting and Sculpture 1940–1970." *Arts Magazine,* Sept.–Oct., p. 35.

Solomon, Alan. "Some Observations about New York Painting," in *Painting in New York: 1944–1969.* Pasadena, Calif.: Pasadena Art Museum.

1970

Bailess, Lynn, and Donnell, Carol. "Jules Olitski," in *Color.* Los Angeles: U.C.L.A. Art Council, pp. 36–40.

Colt, Priscilla. "Some Recent Acquisitions of Contemporary Painting." *The Dayton Art Institute Bulletin,* Mar., p. 11.

———. *Color and Field: 1890–1970.* Catalogue introduction. Buffalo, N.Y.: Albright-Knox Art Gallery.

Fenton, Terry. "In the Galleries–Toronto: The David Mirvish Opening Show." *Arts Canada,* Dec., pp. 57–58.

Geldzahler, Henry. *New York Painting and Sculpture: 1940–1970.* Catalogue introduction. New York: The Metropolitan Museum of Art.

Gouk, Alan. "An Essay on Painting." *Studio International,* Oct., pp. 145–48.

Hilton, Timothy. "Commentary." *Studio International,* Sept., p. 100.

Prokopoff, Stephen S. *Two Genera-*

tions of Color Painting. Catalogue introduction. Philadelphia: Institute of Contemporary Art, University of Pennsylvania.

Rose, Barbara. "The Spiritual in Art." *Vogue,* Jan., p. 76.

Warrum, Richard L. *Painting and Sculpture Today.* Catalogue introduction. Indianapolis, Ind.: Contemporary Art Society and Indianapolis Museum of Art.

Wellesley College Museum. "Jules Olitski," in *Contemporary Painting and Sculpture,* Wellesley, Mass.: Wellesley College Museum, Jewett Art Center.

1971

Baker, Kenneth. "New York: Jules Olitski at Rubin Gallery, N.Y." *Artforum,* May, p. 74.

"Ces douze peintres ont un point commun." *Connaissance des arts,* Mar., p. 132.

Domingo, Willis. "New York Galleries: Jules Olitski at Lawrence Rubin Gallery." *Arts Magazine,* Apr., p. 83.

Greenwood, Michael. "Jules Olitski's Sculpture." *Arts Canada,* Feb.–Mar., p. 62.

Gruen, John. "While There's Life . . ." *New York,* Mar. 29, p. 59.

Mills, Paul C. *Spray.* Catalogue introduction. Santa Barbara, Calif.: Santa Barbara Museum of Art.

Prokopoff, Stephen S. "Color Painting in America." *Art and Artists,* July, p. 22.

Ratcliff, Carter. "Reviews and Previews." *Art News,* Apr., p. 20.

Siegel, Jeanne. "Reviews and Previews: Jules Olitski." *Art News,* Sept., p. 17.

Tucker, Marcia. *The Structure of Color.* Catalogue essay. New York: Whitney Museum of American Art.

1972

Bannard, Walter Darby. "Quality, Style

and Olitski." *Artforum*, Oct., pp. 64–67.

Carpenter, Ken. "On Order in the Paintings of Jules Olitski." *Art International*, Dec., pp. 26–30.

Elderfield, John. "Abstract Painting in the Seventies." *Art International*, Summer, pp. 92–94.

———. "Painterliness Redefined: Jules Olitski and Recent Abstract Art, Part I." *Art International*, Dec., pp. 22–25.

Matthias, Rosemary. "In the Galleries: Jules Olitski at Rubin." *Arts Magazine*, Summer, p. 56.

Moffett, Kenworth. *Abstract Painting in the Seventies: A Selection*. Catalogue introduction. Boston: Museum of Fine Arts.

Siegel, Jeanne. "Reviews and Previews: Jules Olitski." *Art News*, Summer, p. 56.

Wilkin, Karen. *Masters of the Sixties*. Catalogue introduction. Edmonton, Alta.: Edmonton Art Gallery.

Zemans, Joyce. "Olitski: The David Mirvish Gallery." *Arts Canada*, Oct.–Nov. p. 67.

1973

Baker, Kenneth. "Olitski: Lavish Failure, Splendid Success." *The Boston Phoenix*, Apr. 24, 3rd sect., pp. 1, 11.

Carpenter, Ken. "Footsteps of a master: the Jules Olitski retrospective." *Studio International*, Sept., pp. 77–79.

Elderfield, John. "Painterliness Redefined: Jules Olitski and Recent Abstract Art, Part II." *Art International*, Apr., pp. 36–41, 101.

———. "Into History." *Studio International*, Nov., pp. 206–208.

Garrelt, Robert. "Jules Olitski in Retrospect" (based on an interview with Jules Olitski). *Sunday Herald Advertiser* (Boston), Apr. 29, p. 42.

Genauer, Emily. "Art and the Artist." *New York Post*, May 19, p. 34.

———. "Art and the Artist." *New York Post*, Sept.

Greenberg, Clement. "Influences of Matisse." *Art International*, Nov., pp. 28–39.

Hess, Thomas B. "Olitski Without Flattery." *New York*, Oct. 1, pp. 76–77.

Hoesterey, Ingeborg. "Die traditionellen Medien, Uberwiegen, Zum Auschlub de New Yorker Kunstsaison, 1972/3." *Suddeutschezeitung*, no. 169, p. 12.

Hohmeyer, Dr. Jursen. "Lockere Hand, Das Tafelbild lebt auf Prospect 73 die Trend-Schau de saison, demonstrient, dass Kunstler auch heute malen." *Der Spiegel*, Oct., pp. 178–80.

Hughes, Robert. "Art." *Time*, July 16.

Kramer, Hilton. "Art: Jules Olitski Retrospective." *The New York Times*, Sept. 8.

———. "Jules Olitski: A Sectarian Scenario." *The New York Times*, Sept. 16.

Kelly, Mary Lou. "Olitski Retrospective: An Infatuation with Color." *The Christian Science Monitor*, Apr. 12, p. 11.

Lasky, Nora. "Art: Monuments and Minimalism." *The Real Paper* (Boston), Apr. 25, p. 19.

Littman, Sol. "Nailing Down Artistic Success." *The Toronto Star*, Oct. 12, p. E8.

———. "World Famous Art Masters Open Exhibits in Toronto." *The Toronto Star*, Oct. 16.

Loercher, Diana. "Olitski and His Unique Contribution: A Major Display, a Talk with the Artist." *The Christian Science Monitor*, Sept. 15, Arts and Entertainment section, and "No Great Art Without Character says Olitski." Sept. 17.

Masheck, Joseph. "The Jules Olitski Retrospective." *Artforum*, Sept., pp. 56–60.

Moffett, Kenworth. "Jules Olitski and the State of the Easel Painting." *Arts Magazine*, Mar., pp. 42–48.

Reeves, Jean. "Olitski's Shimmer, Vi-brate with Mists of Color, Transparent Paint." *Buffalo Evening News*, June 4.

———. "Artist Olitski Advocates Risky Road to Success." *Buffalo Evening News*, June 16.

[Review]. "Exhibit at Mirvish Gallery, Toronto." *Artscanada*, Dec., p. 196.

Rosenberg, Harold. "The Art World, Dogma and Talent." *The New Yorker*, Oct. 15, pp. 113–19.

Sheridan, Less. "Hub 20th Century Exhibit Retrospective of Olitski's Art." *Springfield Daily News* (Springfield, Mass.), Apr. 19.

Siegel, Jeanne. "Olitski's Retrospective: Infinite Variety." *ARTnews*, Summer, pp. 61–63.

Toupin, Gilles. "Superman et la peinture." *La Presse* (Montreal), Nov. 10.

1974

Baker, Kenneth. "New York Exhibition at Knoedler's Contemporary." *Art in America*, Mar., pp. 106–107.

Bannard, Walter Darby. "Morris Louis and the Restructured Picture." *Studio International*, July–Aug., pp. 18–20.

Carmean, E. A., Jr. "Modernist Art: 1960 to 1970." *Studio International*, July–Aug., pp. 9–15.

Fenton, Terry. "Larry Poons: Recent Paintings." *Art Spectrum*, Jan., pp. 30–40.

Geelhaar, Christian. "Jules Olitski." *Kunstforum International*, Oct–Nov., pp. 113–21.

Henning, E. B. "Jules Olitski and *Omsk Measure II*." *Cleveland Museum Bulletin*, Sept. pp. 233–39.

Hudson, Andrew. *Jules Olitski: Life Drawings*. Catalogue introduction. Washington, D. C.: Corcoran Gallery of Art.

"Jules Olitski." *ARTnews*, Jan., p. 93.

McCaughey, Patrick. "Sydney Ball." *Art International*, Oct., pp. 50–51.

Millard, Charles. "Jules Olitski." *Hudson Review*, Oct., pp. 401–408.

Nasgaard, Raould. "Jules Olitski at the David Mirvish Gallery, Toronto." *Arts Magazine*, Nov., p. 23.

Thompson, B. "The Strange Case of Jules Olitski." *Art in America*, Jan., pp. 62–63.

Wilkin, Karen. "Dan Christensen: Recent Paintings." *Art International*, Summer, pp. 57–58.

1975

Bach, Friedrich. "Interview mit Jules Olitski." *Kunstwerk*, May, pp. 14–24.

Bourdon, David, "You Can't Tell a Painter by His Colors." *The Village Voice*, Mar. 24, p. 94.

Carmean, E. A. "Olitski, Cubism and Transparency." *Arts Magazine*, Nov., pp. 53–57.

Ellenzweig, Allen. "Jules Olitski." *Arts Magazine*, June, p. 10.

Hoesterey, Ingeborg. "New York." *Art International*, June 15, pp. 72–73.

———. "Corten-Stahl ist das material de plastik der Siebziger Jahre." *Art International*, Dec., pp. 46–48.

Hudson, Andrew. "Washington Letter." *Art International*, June 15, pp. 92–97.

———. "Jules Olitski: Life Drawings." *Art International*, Sept. 15, pp. 39–49.

Overy, Paul. "The Arts, Symbols of Technological Faith." *The Times* (London) June 9.

Robbins, Daniel. "Biennials." (review of Whitney Biennial and Corcoran Gallery of Art's 34th Biennial). *New Republic*.

Vaizey, Marina. "Seductive Features." *The Sunday Times* (London), June 8.

1976

Burnett, D. "Jules Olitski, David Mirvish Gallery, Toronto." *Arts Canada*, Oct., pp. 66–67.

Frackman, Noel. "Jules Olitski." *Arts Magazine*, June, p. 29.

Henry, Gerrit. "Views from the Studio."

ARTnews, May, p. 32.

Hoesterey, Ingeborg. "New York." *Art International,* Summer, pp. 32–33.

1977

Baker, Kenneth. "Jules Olitski Shifts Ground." *The Boston Phoenix,* May 10. sect. 3, pp. 1, 14.

Forgey, Benjamin. "Some Additions to the Sculptural." *Washington Star,* July 31.

Giuliano, Charles. "Interview with Olitski." *The Boston Phoenix,* May 10, sect. 3, pp. 1, 14.

Glueck, Grace. "The 20th Century Artists · Most Admired by Other Artists." *ARTnews,* Nov., p. 78.

Moffett, Kenworth. *Kenneth Noland.* New York: Harry N. Abrams.

Saulnier, Bonny. "As a Painter Sure, as a Sculptor Maybe." *The Patriot Ledger* (Boston), May 26, p. 48.

1978

Ashbery, John. "Cheering Up Our Knowing." *New York,* Apr. 10, pp. 69–71.

Frackman, Noel. "Reviews." *Arts Magazine,* June, pp. 36–37.

Hudson, Andrew. "Sculptors in Steel Around Bennington." *Bennington Review,* Dec., pp. 55–69.

Maloon, Terence. *Time Out* (London), Apr. 28.

Marshall, Neil. *Jules Olitski, New Paintings.* Catalogue essay. New York: André Emmerich Gallery.

McEwen, John. *Spectator* (London), Apr. 22.

Moffett, Kenworth. "Olitski: New Sculpture." *Art International,* Mar., pp. 8–21.

Perreault, John. *Selected 20th Century American Nudes.* Catalogue essay. New York: Harold Reed Gallery.

Raynor, Vivien. "Art: Jules Olitski as Post-Raphaelite." *The New York Times,* Mar. 31.

Schjeldahl, Peter. "Jules Olitski." *Artforum,* Summer, pp. 69–70.

Schwartz, Ellen. "Jules Olitski." *ARTnews,* Summer, p. 198.

Welish, Marjorie. "Jules Olitski." *Art in America,* Sept., pp. 119–20.

1979

Fenton, Terry. "Jules Olitski and the Tradition of Oil Painting," in *Jules Olitski: Paintings of the 1970s.* Edmonton, Alta: Edmonton Art Gallery.

Moffett, Kenworth. *Color Abstractions.* Catalogue essay. Boston: Federal Reserve Bank.

1980

Pleynet, Marcellin. "Jules Olitski: The Challenge of Abstraction." *Connaissance des Arts* (U. S. edition), Oct., pp. 66–71.

1981

Fourcade, Michael. "Pour une nouvelle respiration." Catalogue essay. Bordeaux, France: CAPC, pp. 3–10.

PHOTOCREDITS

Numerals refer to plate numbers

Jonathan Barber, North Bennington, Vt.: 192, 194

Brompton Studio, London, England: 64

The Carnegie Institute, Pittsburgh, Pa.: 47

Atelier Eidenberg, Basel, Switzerland: 77

André Emmerich Gallery, New York: 88, 91, 131, 133

French & Company, Inc., New York: 36

Jane Courtney Frisse, Syracuse, N.Y.: 210

Elizabeth Galt: 180, 184

Greg Heims, Boston, Mass.: 72, 92, 96, 130

Hickey-Robertson, Houston, Tex.: 73

Scott Hyde, New York: 121

Karol Ike: 93, 111

Seth Joel, New York: 50, 53, 54, 62, 115

E. Lazare: 60

Bruce C. Jones: 136, 139, 141–43, 198–202, 228

Stuart Lisson, Syracuse, N.Y.: 208, 209, 224

Helen Miljakovich, New York: 144, 195, 196, 226

Kenworth Moffett: 43–45, 65, 83, 87, 90

Ugo Mulas, Milan, Italy: 211

The Museum of Fine Arts, Boston, Mass.: 193

O.E. Nelson, New York: 41, 42, 94, 114, 119, 123, 134

Jules Olitski: 190

Eric Pollitzer, Garden City Park, N.Y.: 151, 152

Quiriconi-Tropea, Chicago, Ill.: 61

George Roos, New York: 5, 9–12, 19, 20, 27, 28, 30, 31, 33–35, 38, 39, 46, 48, 49, 55, 63, 66, 67, 69, 70, 78–80, 105–107

Georges Routhier, Paris, France: 124

David Smith: 203

Rick Stafford, Harvard University News Office, Cambridge, Mass.: 225

John R. Tennant, Mt. Airy, Md.: 125, 128

Frank J. Thomas, Los Angeles, Calif.: 112

Malcolm Varon, New York: 103

Cora Kelly Ward, New York: 222

Bernard Williams, The Corcoran Gallery of Art, Washington, D.C.: 138, 140

INDEX

Italic numerals refer to plates